MIKAN
Save the Danchi
Mass Estates–A Project of the Future

a:p architektur:positionen

jovis

Table of contents

introduction

READ THE DANCHI 006

manual

MANUAL 008 PROCESS 010 INDEX 012
OPERATION 014 GENRE 016

item

ITEM 001–077 018

001 Park Park /002 Sports Park /003 Mushroom Wall /004 Fruits Park /005 Spaghetti /006 Golden Pavilion /007 Flower Parking /008 Just a bit Public / 009 Related to Public /010 Very Public /011 Top Room /012 Top Pool /013 Top Per /014 Top Gard /015 Top Con /016 Rain House /017 Top Mesh /018 Top Res /019 Bill Buil /020 Botanical Face /021 Sun Sun Sun /022 Taishin Finishing /023 Cheese /024 Art Wall /025 Cinema Wall /026 Eyes /027 Cube / 028 House Heat /029 Exchange /030 Short Cut /031 Market /032 Hall in Hole / 033 Air Park /034 Floating Room /035 Office Service /036 Stories of Balconies / 037 Blooming in the Stairs /038 Cover Up /039 Stairs In, Stairs Out /040 Ceiling Up /041 Co Bath /042 Co Kitchen /043 Rain Bath /044 Door to Door /045 Flush the Flowers /046 Danchi Block /047 SOHO /048 Rest the Guests /049 Atelier Danchi /050 High-Rise Garden /051 Private Garden /052 Mail-Go-Round /053 Box in Box /054 Recycled Billboard /055 Sanit Unit /056 Sign House /057 Cover Tower /058 Under Cover /059 Zoo Balcony /060 Big Bal /061 My Beautiful Balcony /062 Baroom /063 Kit Cut /064 Mind the Curtains /065 Outer Dryer /066 Full Open Window /067 Rolling Dryer /068 Passive I /069 Shop & Door /070 Living Module System /071 Domani /072 Foot On /073 Foam Wall /074 Fish Wall /075 Peep Show /076 Danchi Eye /077 www.danchi

about MIKAN 172

READ THE DANCHI

Origins

The Japanese word danchi may not be evocative for a foreign reader, though its present meaning—which appeared in the mid-nineteen-fifties—became common language here. At that time, with the rebirth of its economy, Japan began a mass-housing policy of shugojyutakudanchi (collective housing estates) summarized in the shorter and popular danchi. Even though modern collective housings appeared in Japan in the nineteen-twenties, danchi was a post-war phenomenon linked with the need to respond quickly to a large increase in the urban population due to the baby-boom, the rising of the industrial production, and the rural exodus. Thus, these estates epitomize for many Japanese this period of harsh renewal.

Whites Slabs-Green Carpets

By 1955, semipublic institutions in charge of the construction of the danchi were establishing standards both for the types and surfaces of the apartment units and the site planning of the blocks themselves. Conditions were rather drastic with an average flat called a 2DK (2 bedrooms, a living and a dining room) of only forty-three square meters. Several kinds of housing units were also developed, the most common one being a bare concrete slab of four or five stories with series of outer staircases connecting two flats at each level and no elevator. Later, housing units exceeding ten stories were built with outer corridors at each level connecting all the flats with fewer staircases.
All of these estates, which were made out of repetitive and archetypal housing units, summarize modernist urbanity: series of parallel slabs set up in large open space and oriented towards the south like sunflowers (balconies and main rooms—living/dining and main bedroom—towards the south, while other bedrooms and access—exterior staircases and corridors—face the north). Similar in their aims and bareness to Western examples of large collective housings, they continued to be built until the early nineteen-eighties. At that time, new kinds of mansions and individual housings built mainly by the private sector took over the danchi.

Potentiality

If one considers this post-war heritage, one certainly has dubious feelings. Such bareness may seem like the sad son of both modern planning and economic constraints of the period. However, contrary to the rejection of its American and European counterparts, Japanese danchi, though nowadays considered obsolete, have rarely been a subject of fear and hard criticism. This fate tends to be explained by various factors. First of all, one has to consider the Japanese population's high level of civility. The danchi, though repetitive and cheaply made, have never been trashed or subject to violence. On the contrary, the first owners often stayed and organized lively communities. Moreover, large Japanese towns show a much more informal fabric than European ones, allowing a vast repertoire of objects and constructions. City centers do not formally oppose suburbs. Consequently, the latter do not enter in the agenda of social conflicts nor these estates. Danchi, though foreign to the local tradition of low wooden constructions of cities, participated in a larger rejuvenation of post-war Japanese urbanity that started in the eighteen-seventies with the political opening towards the world of previously secluded Japan. Today, they often look like convenient and green oasis within densely built Japanese cities.

A Tribute

Since the late nineteen-nineties, in a country where the average life span of a house is less than twenty-five years, danchi are considered a decaying stock by authorities that destroy and replace them with contemporary versions. Though one does not deny obsolescence and lack of comfort in regard to present needs, one assumes that danchi not only wrote a chapter of modern Japan but still provide places offering affordable and nice environments for living if adapted to changing times. Ultimately, they deserve more than mere eradication. This book is a late homage to the danchi and all their social, architectural, as well as urban potential.

001
Manual

Item
Title for each idea of the catalogue of renovations

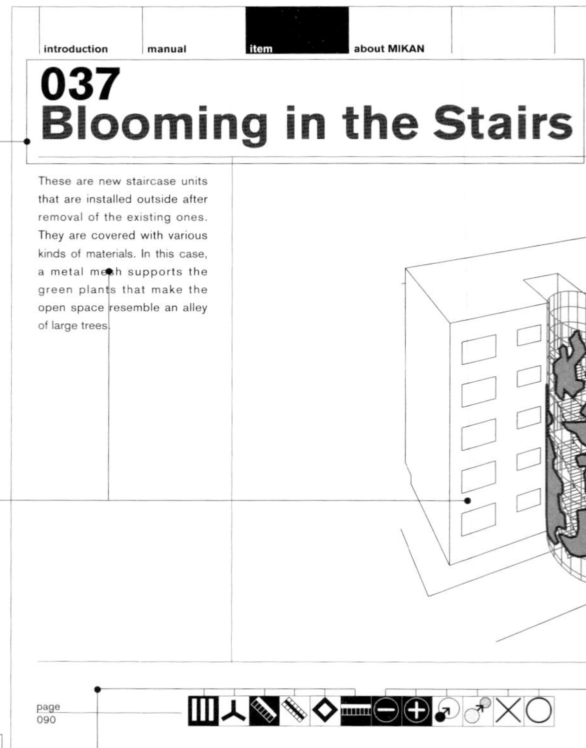

Contents
A sentence and an illustration introduce the basic idea of each item.

Index Icon
These icons describe the types of housing units.

Operation Icon
These icons describe the kinds of physical operations done to a housing unit.

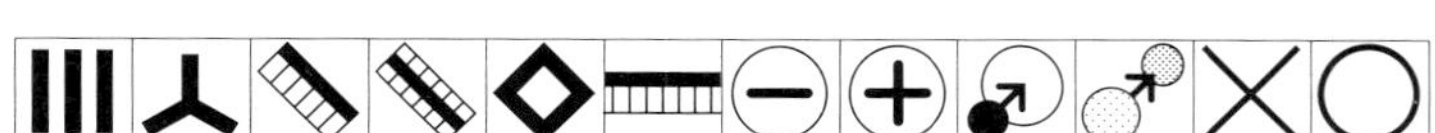

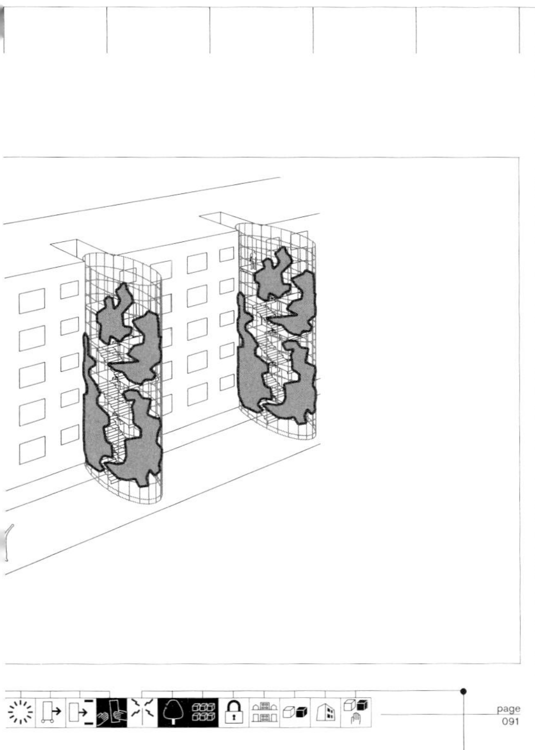

Genre Icon
These icons describe
the types of renovations.

002 Process

This book, organized as a catalogue of ideas, addresses not only the kind of danchi estates that were built in large quantities, but a large variety of housing complexes, too.

This book represents a response to a social demand, though there is a wide range of actions from extremely personal needs (such as safety or comfort of the buildings and the apartments) to more public considerations (such as their appearance within larger estates or even the cities). Visualized as a catalogue, which will be used as an archive that anyone can search, the potential of the existing danchi to satisfy these demands is revealed.

If one uses this catalogue as an archive, a process like the one shown on the right-hand page will take place. Because of the risk that the reproduction of a particular item chosen from this catalogue conveys for the existing estate as a whole, the following process of selection should be implemented. First, an analysis of the conditions of the renovation of the danchi will be made by the planner (the architect). Then the people of the neighborhood association of the housing complex will act as coordinators for the site work. Eventually, the system will allow the residents to pick up concrete items one by one. Moreover, the addition and free selection of items allows the enlargement of the catalogue and prevents any mannerism resulting from the choice.

Ultimately, this catalogue is not a finished piece and should be updated continuously. Thus, through this constant process of reevaluation, the danchi renovation planning will proceed freely.

Catalogue the Renovation of Danchi

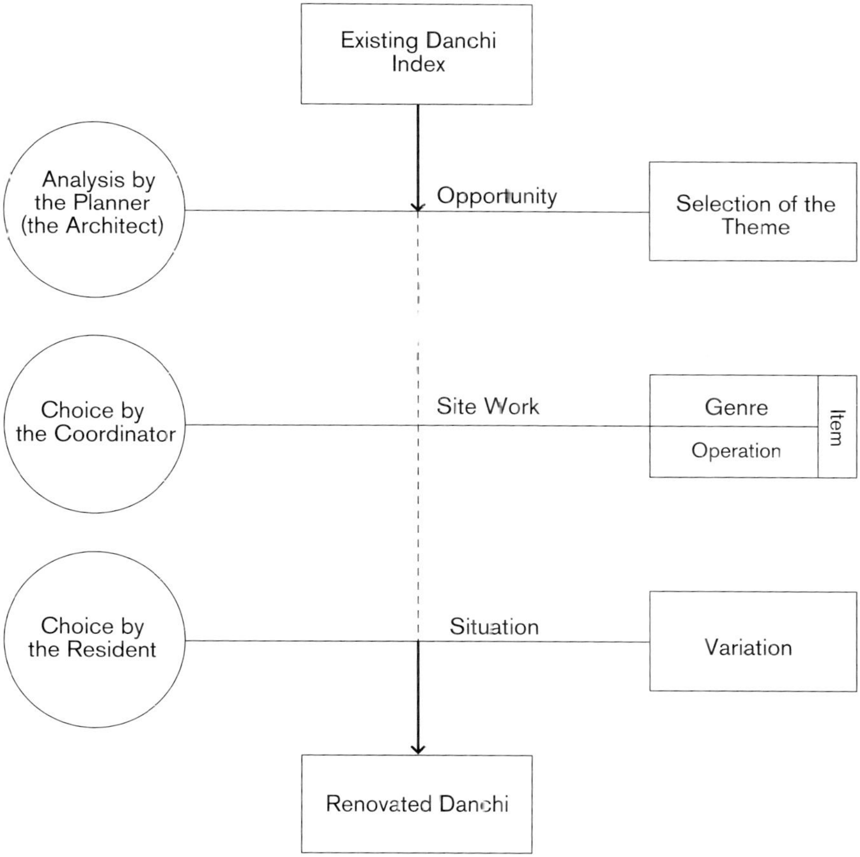

003 Index

Public collective rented housing built from the middle of the nineteen-fifties until the nineteen-seventies is divided into six types. Each of them is represented by an icon that shows the relation between the kind of housing and the catalogue of concrete items.

Medium-rise Danchi Model medium-rise slab type medium-rise tower type
Models of four to five stories offer a relatively low density. In Tokyo, such models are mainly seen in residential areas outside the ring of the Yamanote Line. The structure is made of RC bearing walls. Housing units are homogeneous and offer few variations.
The interval between the buildings is determined by a standardized number of daylight hours at the winter solstice. The tower type (this basic type is star shaped with angles of 120 degrees. The central part is used for the staircase) also clears the daylight standards.
In many danchi, the mixing of tower types mix with battery like ones (a series of parallel medium rise slabs) brings some variety.
Within the medium-rise danchi, the open space, which allows direct sunlight, offers a good space for gardens, though it is often used as a parking lot.
Access to the dwellings is usually by exterior stairways and corridors.

High-rise commercial compound model (exterior corridor type with commerce/inner corridor type with commerce/inner court type with commerce).
Models usually consisting of nine to ten stories are present in many parts of Tokyo within the ring of the Yamanote Line. The structure is made of beams and columns of RC. Usually, the lower part of the building is used for commercial facilities and offices, while dwellings are found above the fourth-floor level. Due to the urban environment, balconies are rare, but in many cases the flat roof is open and used as a common terrace by the inhabitants for drying laundry. Most of the ground floor is occupied by shops that face the main street, and the entrance to the housing is often inconspicuous.

High-rise danchi high-rise type
Twelve-to-fifteen-story buildings are often provided with exterior corridors. These large danchi estates are usually developed by a combination of public and private sectors and offer apartments for rent and sale. Such large-scale housing complexes include a park for the neighborhood. The structure is made of RC or SRC beams and columns. Takashimadaira danchi and Hikarigaoka danchi are representative example of such estates. Commercial facilities (run by tenants) are featured on the ground floor, and parks fill up the space surrounded like a valley by the buildings. Balconies (the older ones have only a small depth) protrude on the south side, while exterior corridors protected from the wind by a fence (made of polycarbonate and tempered glass) are attached to the floors on the north side. Eventually meeting rooms and one word: daycare nurseries are incorporated in the site.

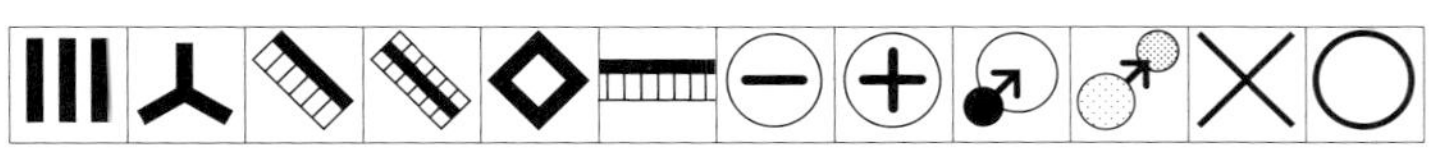

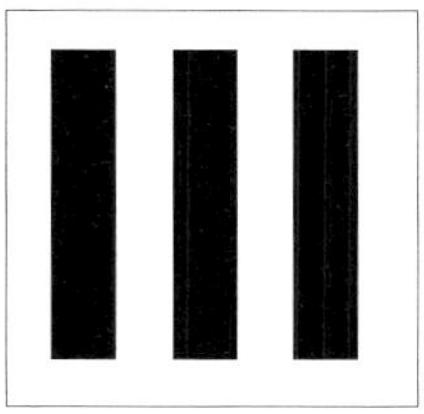

medium-rise slab

medium-rise tower

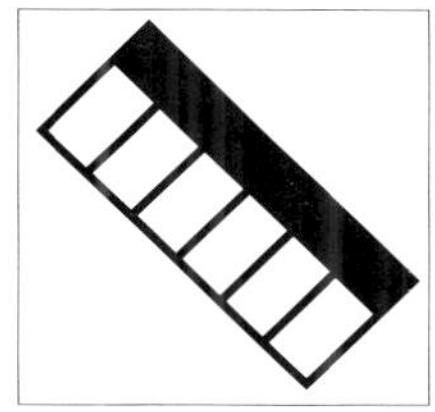

exterior corridor with commerce

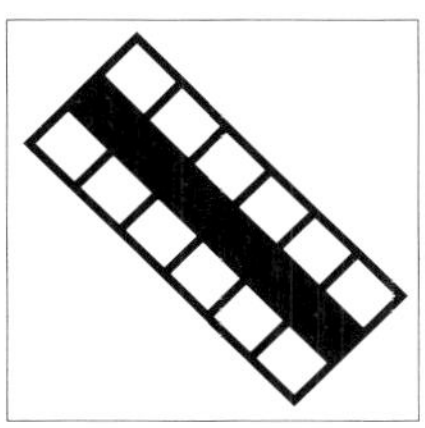

inner corridor with commerce

inner court with commerce

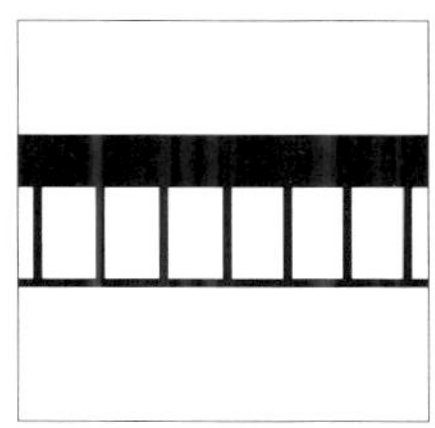

high-rise

004 Operation

As a method of classification, nine basic operations are defined. Each of them is represented by an icon that links one operation to the related item.

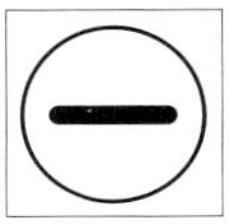

Subtract

Operation to reduce the volume of an existing building, such as the removal of the intermediate floor or the externalization of the ground floor.

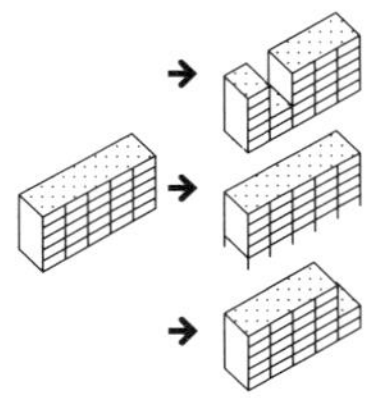

Add

Operation to add a new volume to an existing building.

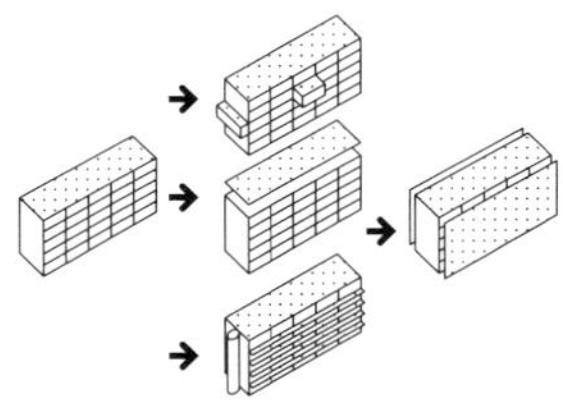

Combine

Operation that combines into a new unit, two or more existing housing units. It is accompanied by the removal of parts such as floors or walls.

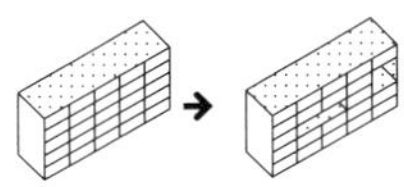

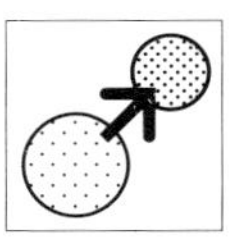

Densify

Operation adding a new volume between existing buildings. This increases their density in the estate.

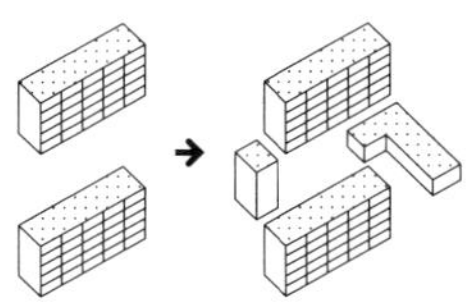

Close

Operation separating the whole building or the site from the outside.

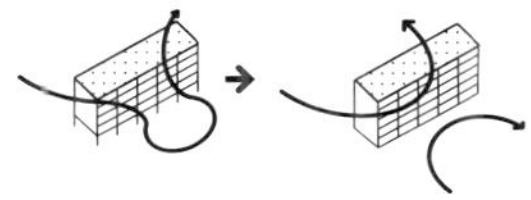

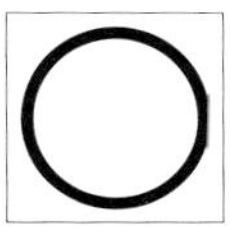

Open

Operation opening the whole building or the site to the community.

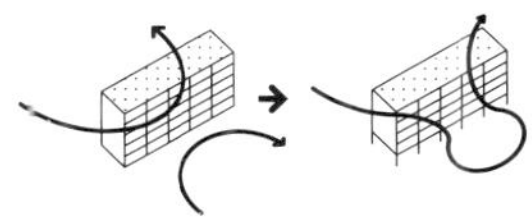

Change

Operation changing the function without physically replacing a building.

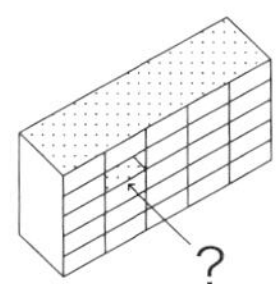

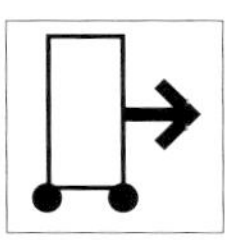

Make mobile

Operation adding a mobile part to a building. This part is flexible and can cope with various functions.

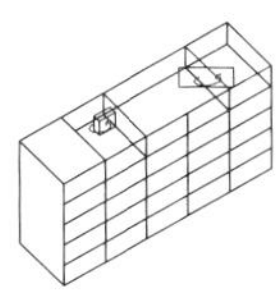

Attach

Operation adding a new device to an existing building.

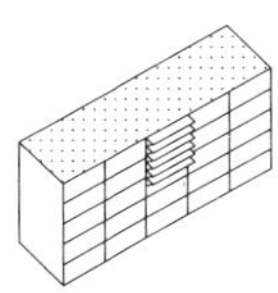

005
Genre

Contents of the renovation have been classified into nine categories or genres. Each of them is represented by an icon that directly illustrates the character of the change.

Service

Addition or renewal of a public service for the residents.

Media

Adding a function that uses visuals or the Internet.

Ecology

Contributing to the environment by effective practical use, or prevention of global warming.

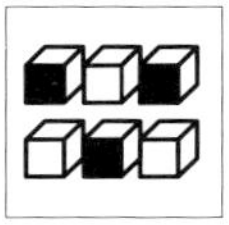

Product

Helping new functions with new products. Development of products.

Security

Protecting the residents by the prevention of danger, crime, or disaster. Crisis control.

Sustainability

Lengthening the life of an existing building.

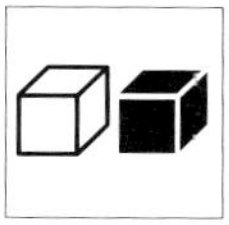

Variation

Changing the type of housing unit. Increasing the variety of choices.

Appearance

Changing the appearance of a building.

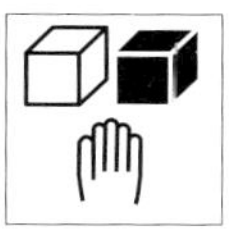

Taste & Habit

Customizing the hobby of each individual inhabitant.

001
Park Park

Parking lots occupy the tight exterior space of the danchi, where one would prefer to enjoy greenery instead. Although there is a need for parking, it should coexist with green, public spaces.
The medium-rise danchi is the perfect place to start a new system offering two types of parking units.
Parking unit A proposes an elevated artificial deck covering the entire parking area.
Parking unit B is based on separate sections. Using existing parking elevators, they are transformed into private terraces.
The result is a double layer in which the lower section caters to the cars, while the upper section provides green spaces for inhabitants.

FRP planting unit

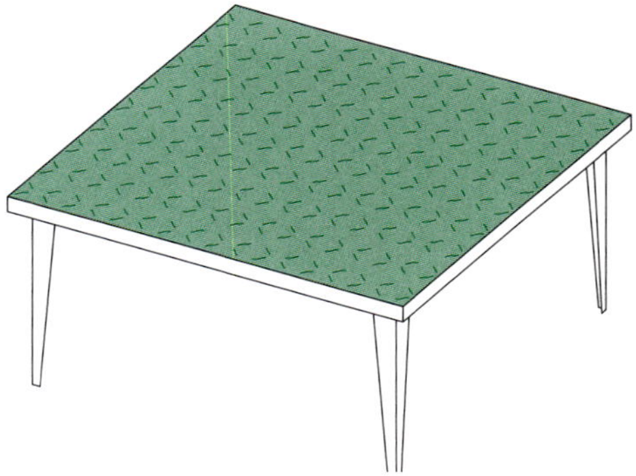

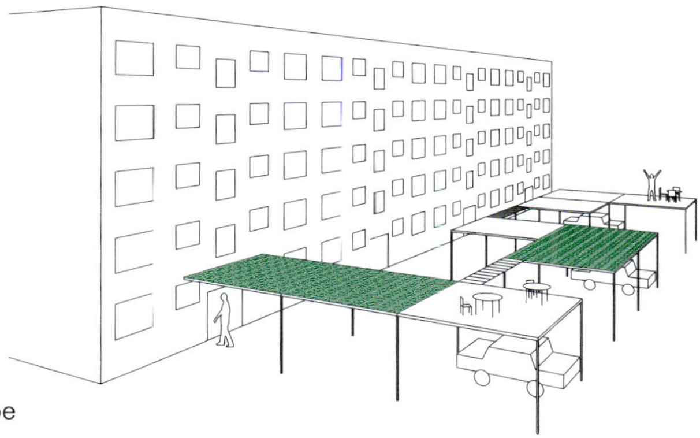

A type

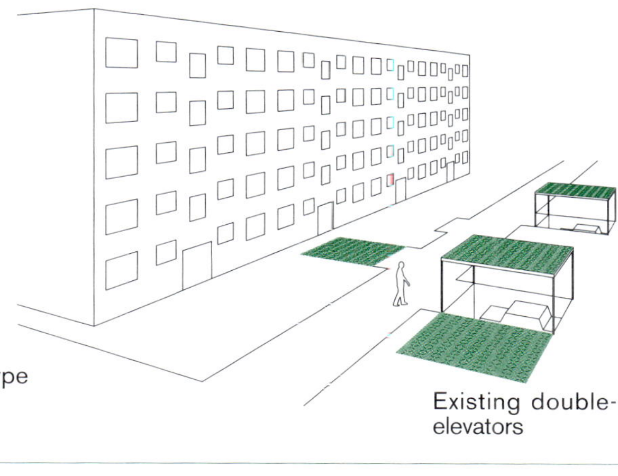

B type

Existing double-decker parking elevators

002
Sports Park

Within densely built cities, the danchi's green, open spaces appear very attractive. These open spaces can be used as parks, which are available to residents as well as neighbors.
A bridge equipped with a track runs through the rich green surroundings.
Additional functions such as a bicycle rack and a gym are incorporated under the track.

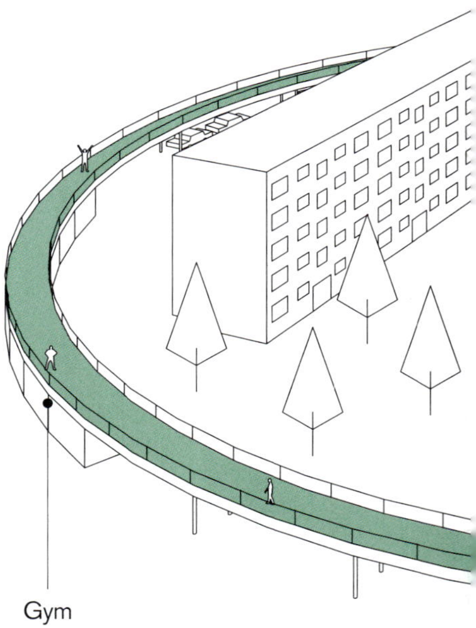

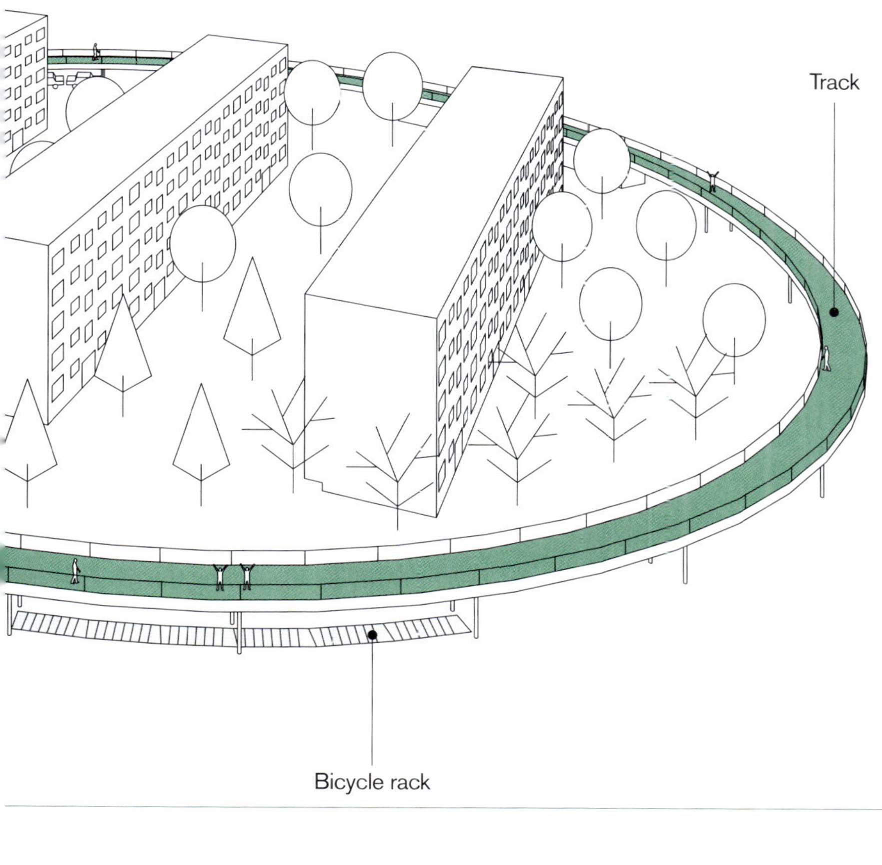
Track
Bicycle rack

003
Mushroom Wall

Since the housings units of the danchi are always oriented towards the south, northern shady spaces appear automatically. These damp places can be used efficiently to grow mushrooms. In addition, firewood needed for cultivating mushrooms creates new landscapes.

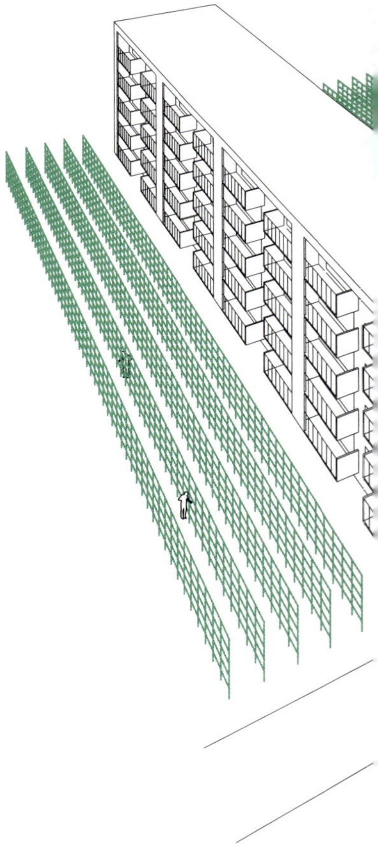

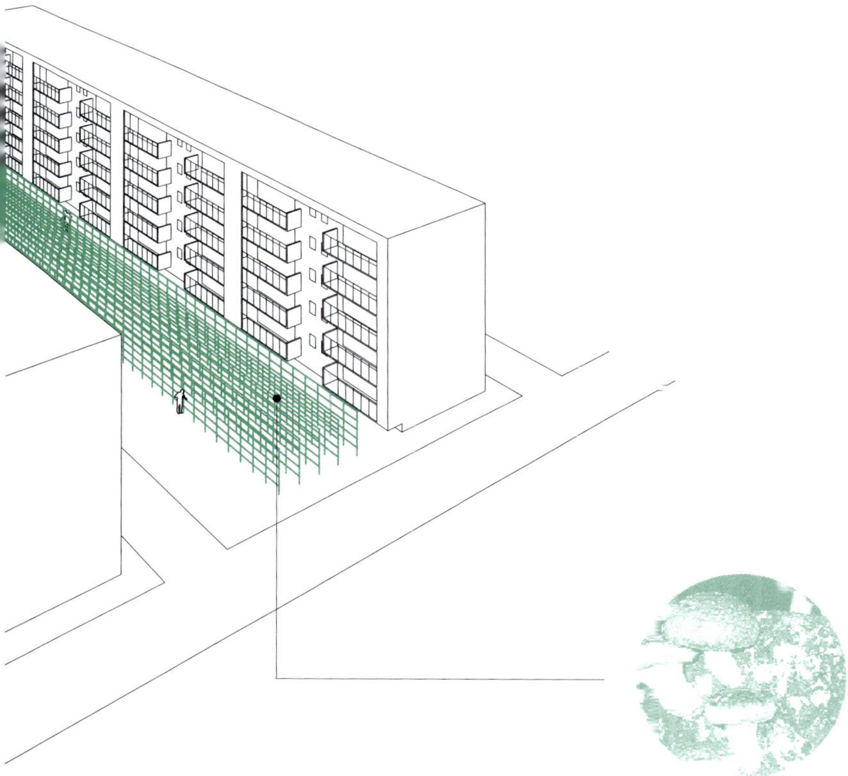

Apart from mushrooms,
morning glories and green
soybeans can also grow here.

004
Fruits Park

The open spaces of the danchi usually offer good exposure to the sun. A wisteria trellis set up on the site creates an orchard where fruits such as pears, grapes, and vegetables can be cultivated. Free access to both residents and neighbors is allowed. Usually, the danchi's open spaces symbolize residents' privacy, but by creating an orchard, the entire neighborhood is taken into account.

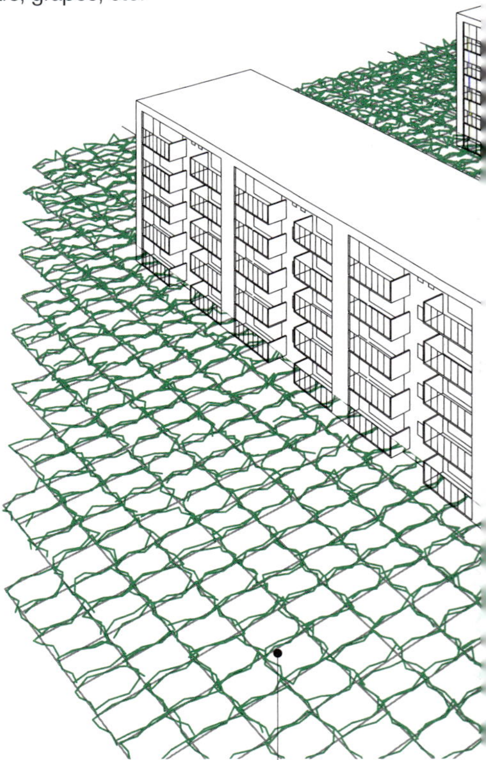

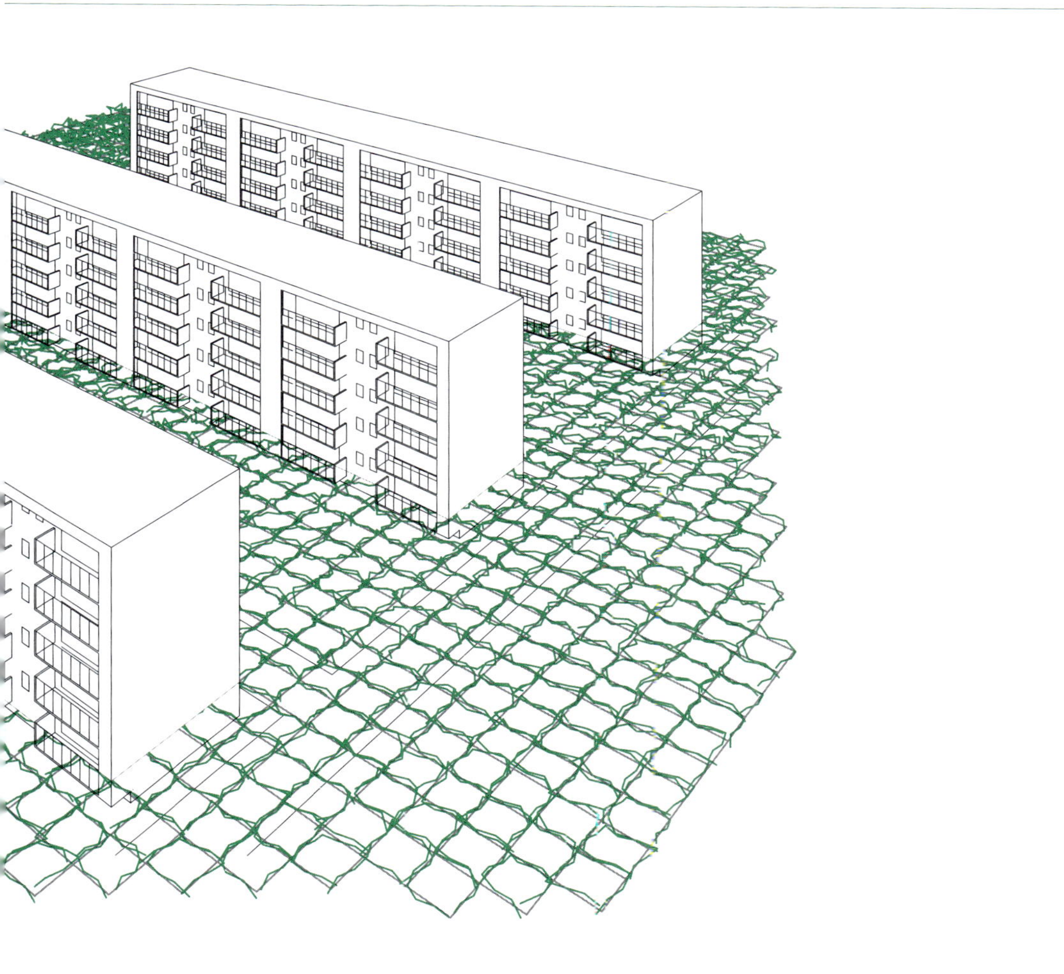

005 Spaghetti

The fact that many danchi have aging populations and are not equipped with elevators providing access to the apartment is a problem, and the placement of elevators is difficult in medium-rise danchi. One solution is to create a slope with barrier-free access. It has a gentle incline with a maximum ratio of 1/18 and features both non-slippery floors and handrails. In addition, such a slope helps encourage activity by joining all of the slab units.

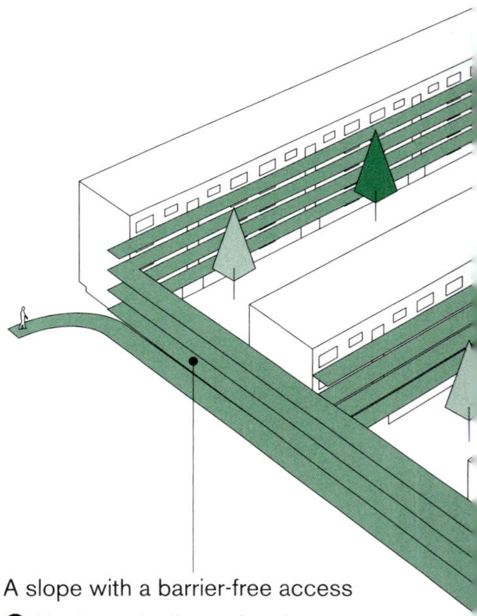

A slope with a barrier-free access

- Maximum incline ratio 1/18
- Non-slippery floor surface and handrails

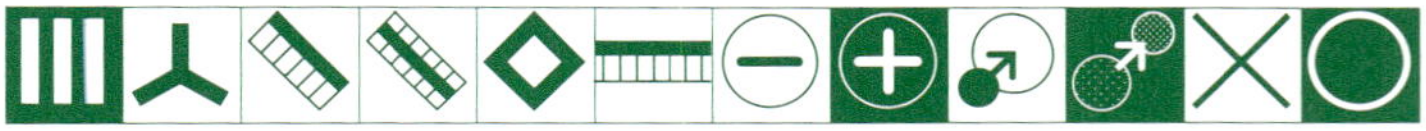

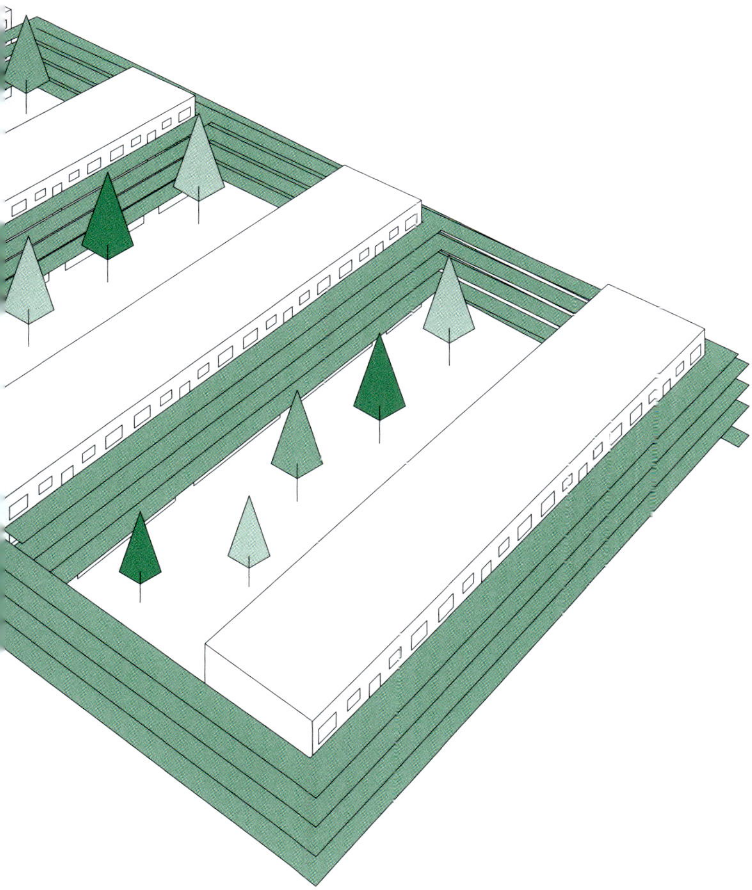

006
Golden Pavilion

This is a suggestion for transforming the open space of a danchi into a pond that surrounds the housing units. Once cleared, the ground floor of each building reveals an open space with piles resembling a pavilion floating on a pond. This space also provides access to the dwellings since the cars can pass through it. The pond will reduce heat in the summer, prevent drying during the winter, and also create landscapes with pleasant humidity. Furthermore, the pond could be used as a possible reservoir.

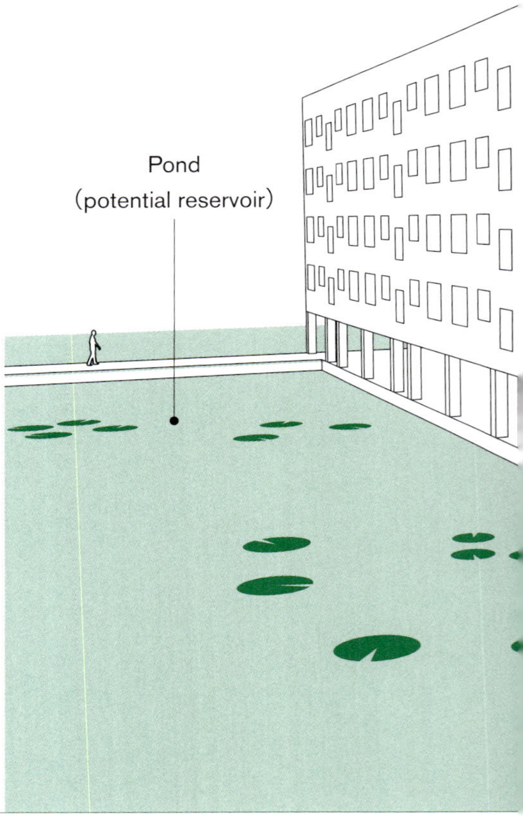

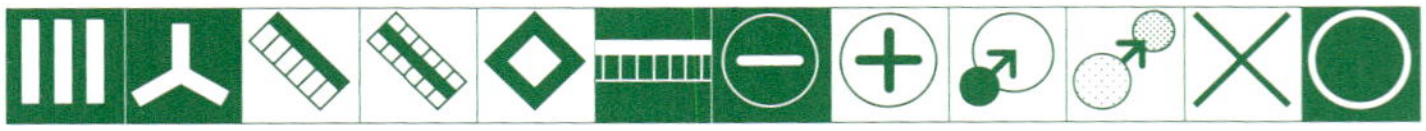

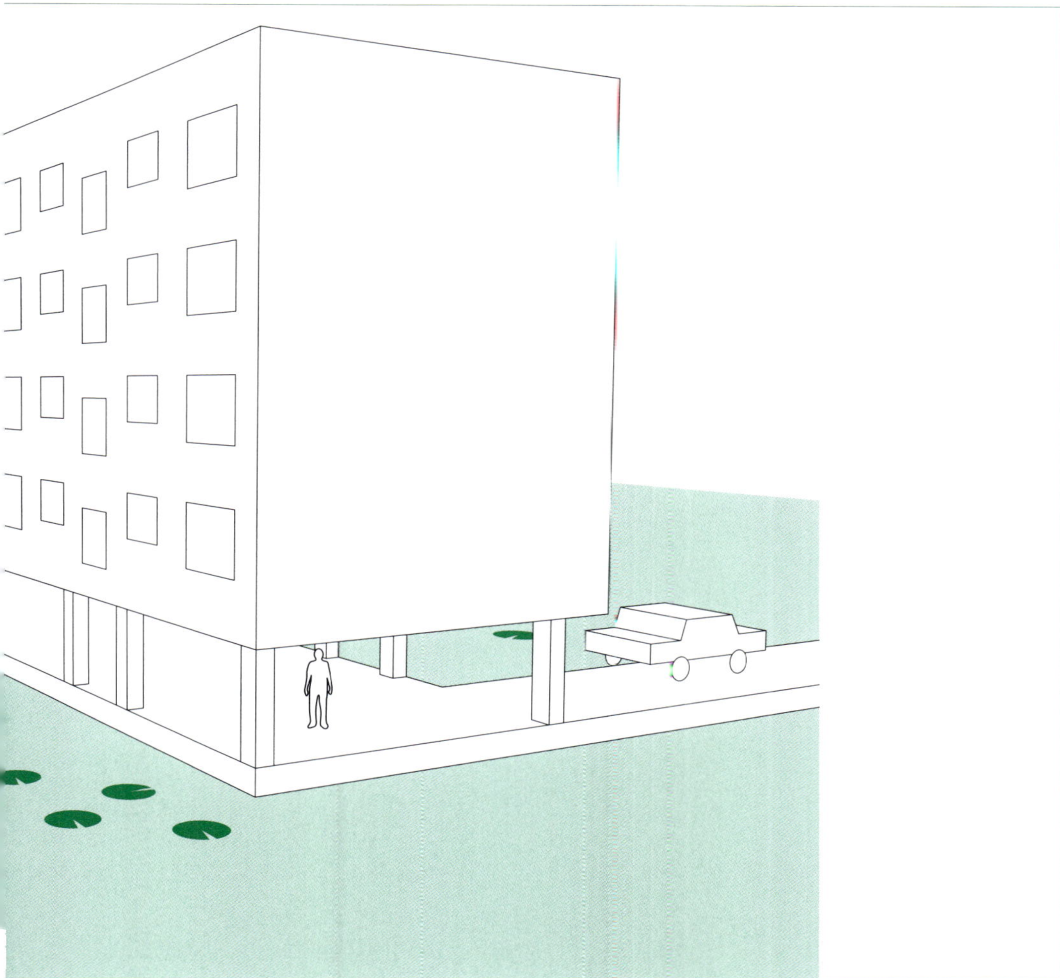

007
Flower Parking

In the danchi's bicycle parking lots, the relationship with the neighboring environment is not usually considered. But it is possible to look at such spaces with a more positive attitude. A roof system that supports growing plants is implemented in harmony with the surrounding trees.

008
Just a bit Public

Housing units in the form of slabs strongly divide the danchi site. However, the removal of the buildings' ground floors and their transformation into spaces with piles bring a feeling of fluid continuity to the entire site. Adding entrance halls, small stores, and other functions needed by the neighborhood and requested by the residents, will encourage new activities.

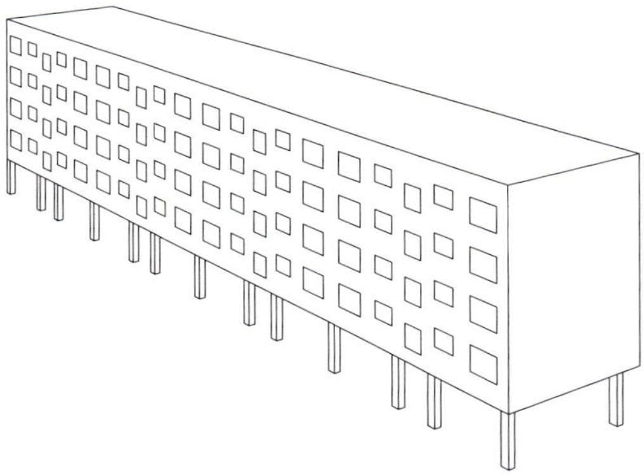

Opening of the ground floor

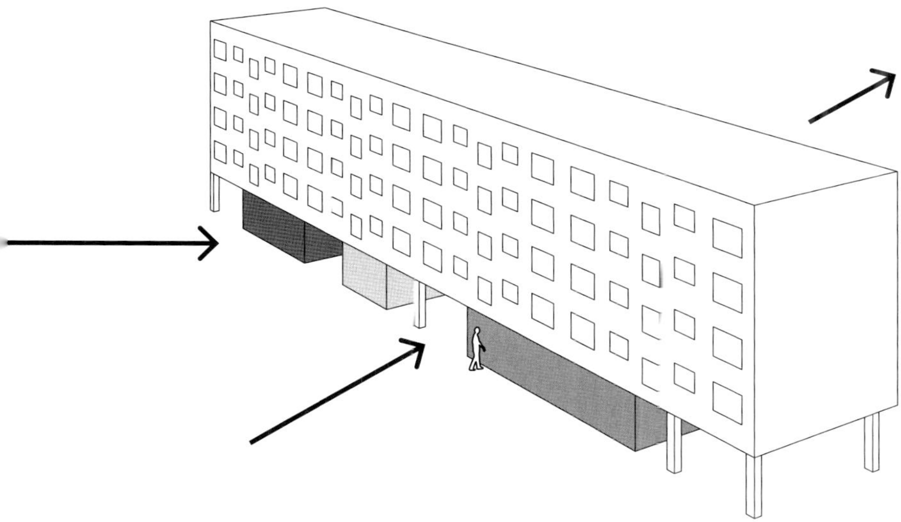

Addition of an entrance hall and a store while maintaining openness

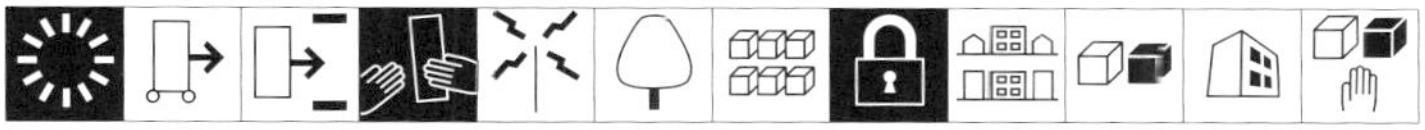

009
Related to Public

Removing the volume of the ground floor of the housing units, brings a feeling of continuity to the entire site. Adding promenades gives a sense of unity by binding together the public space. Moreover, the piles are extended by the construction of an artificial ground next to the block unit. The new setting cultivates activity.

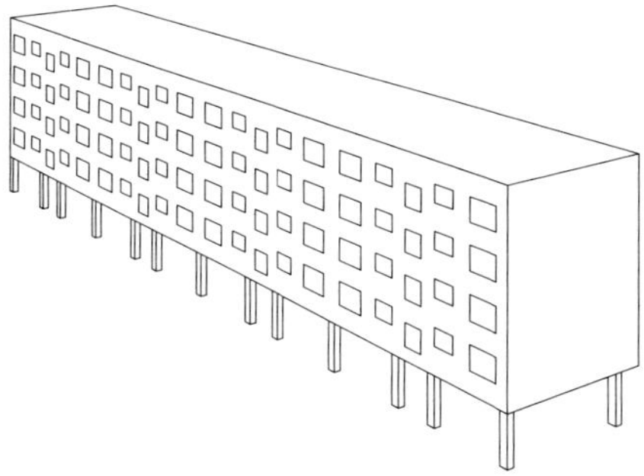

Opening of the ground floor

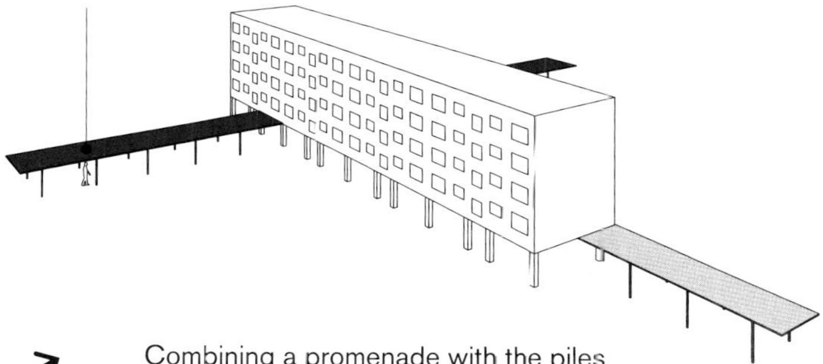

Combining a promenade with the piles

Combining an artificial ground with the piles

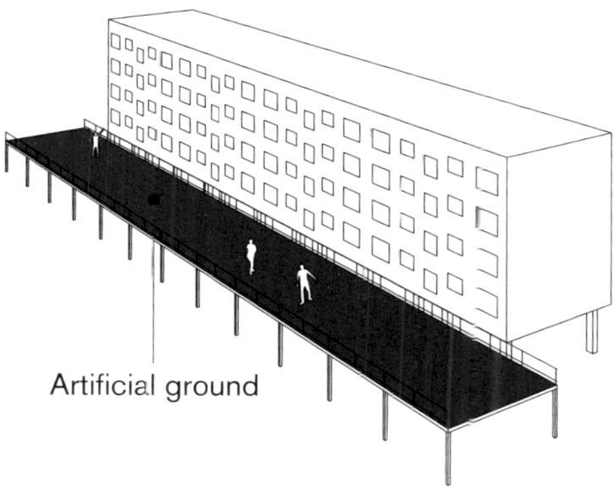

010
Very Public

A nursery school and a daycare center are built after clearing the ground floor of the housing units. These new additions expand into the space between the divided buildings joining them together and creating an entirely new, comprehensive, and active territory.

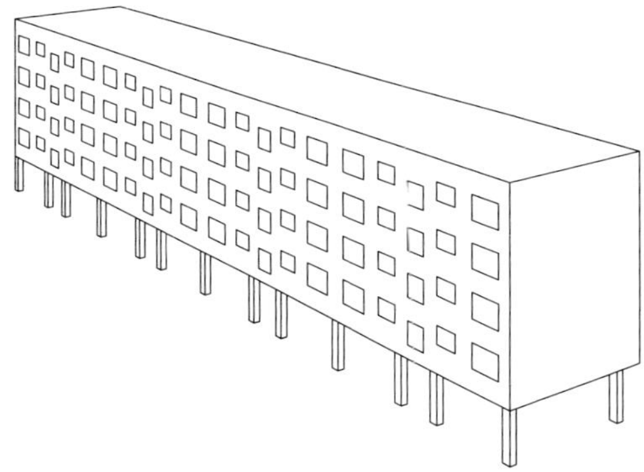

Housing unit with its ground floor cleared

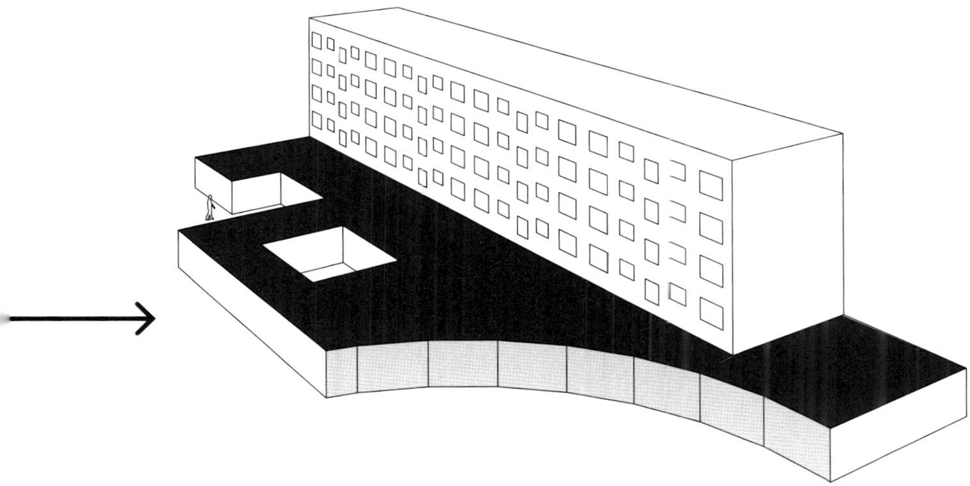

The room under the piles houses a daycare center and a nursery school interlacing organica ly

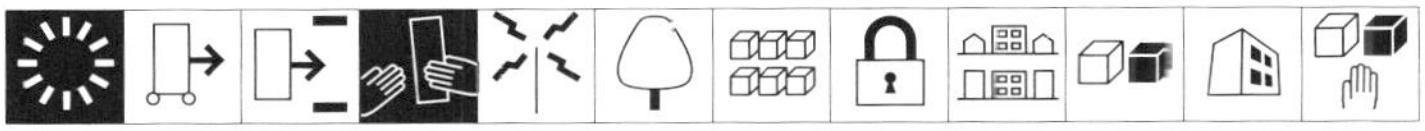

011
Top Room

A small volume is set up on the roof of a housing unit. Structurally, it helps to reinforce inner columns and it can also renew the image of the building with its alien appearance. The enlargement can be used for various purposes—including, meeting place, nursery school, cafe, restaurant, etc.—according to the residents' needs.

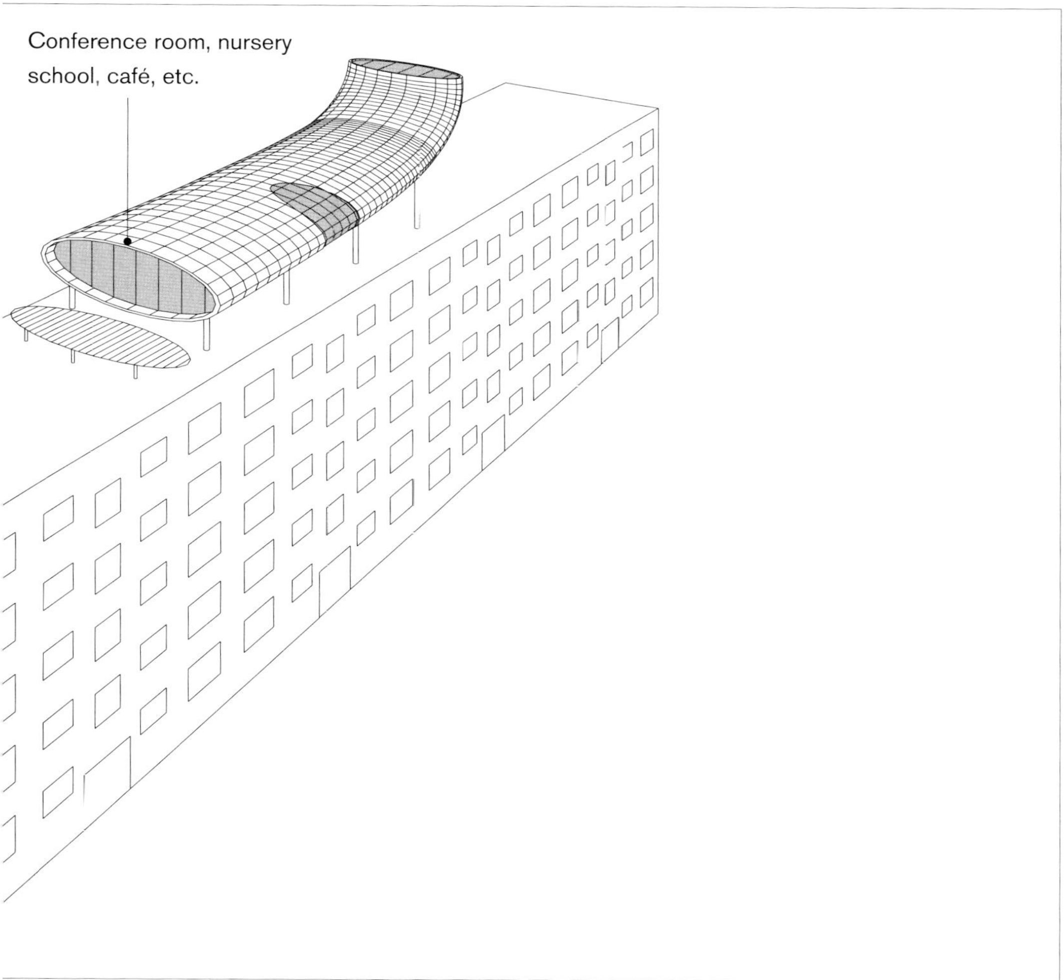
Conference room, nursery
school, café, etc.

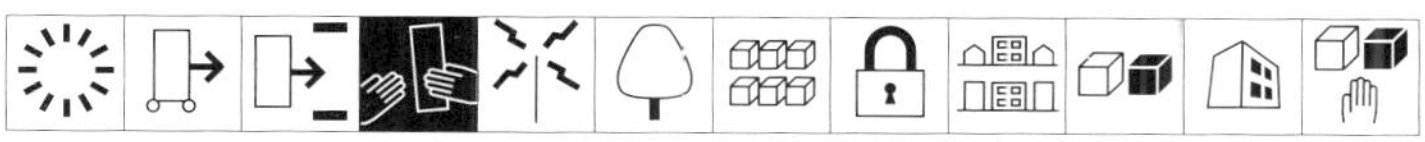

012
Top Pool

A swimming pool is added to the roof of a housing unit. The heavy load of the pool's water requires a new structure, which is implemented on the circumference of the existing building. The new structure supports the hanging extensions of living rooms. The water in the pool can also be used for fire prevention or as a bird sanctuary during the non-summer months.

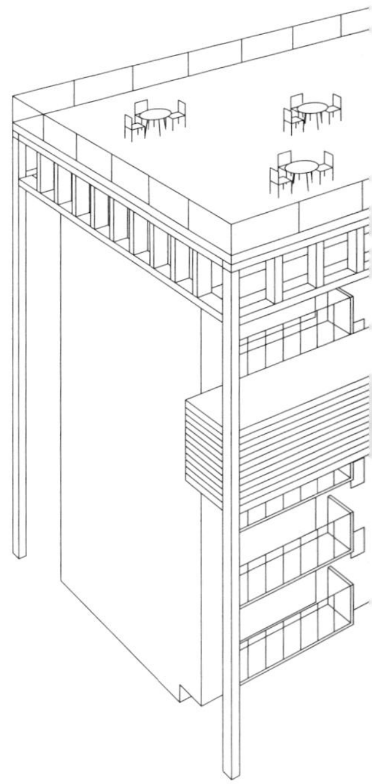

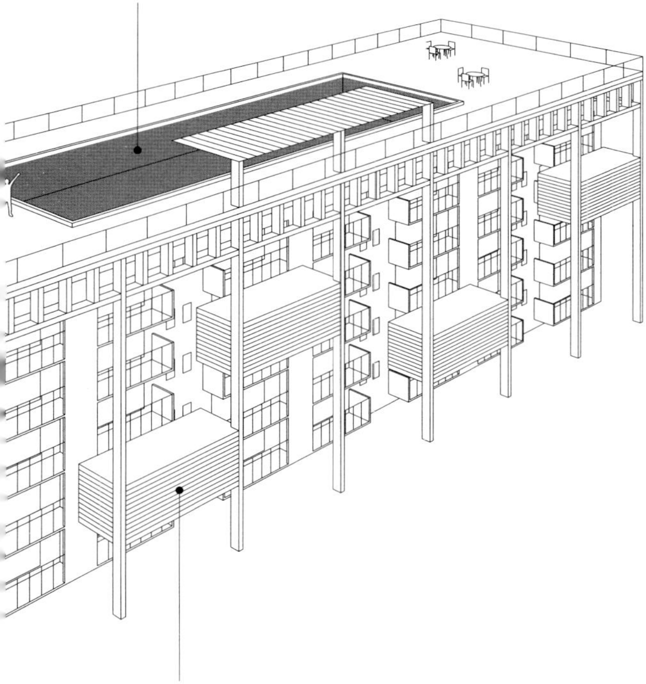
Used as a pool in summer or as a water tank for fire prevention
Possible enlargement of living rooms

013
Top Per

The surface of the roof is covered with a large green platform where plants can grow. This new space offers inhabitants an observatory or open space dotted with pergolas. Rooftop planting is also an effective insulation device.

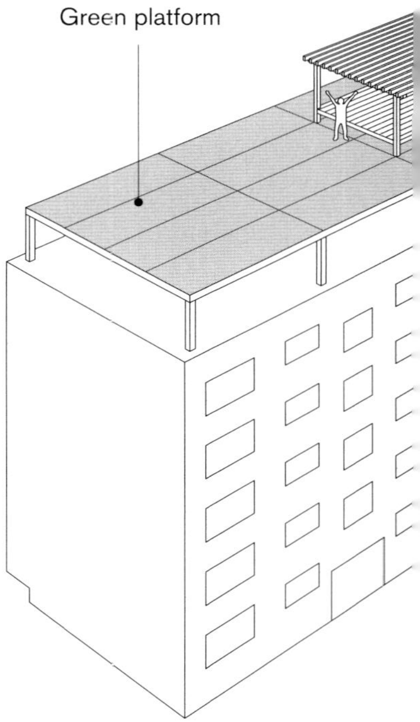

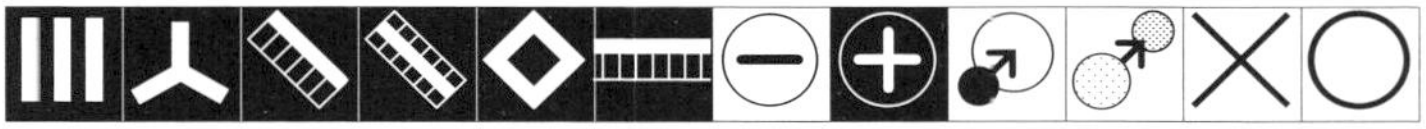

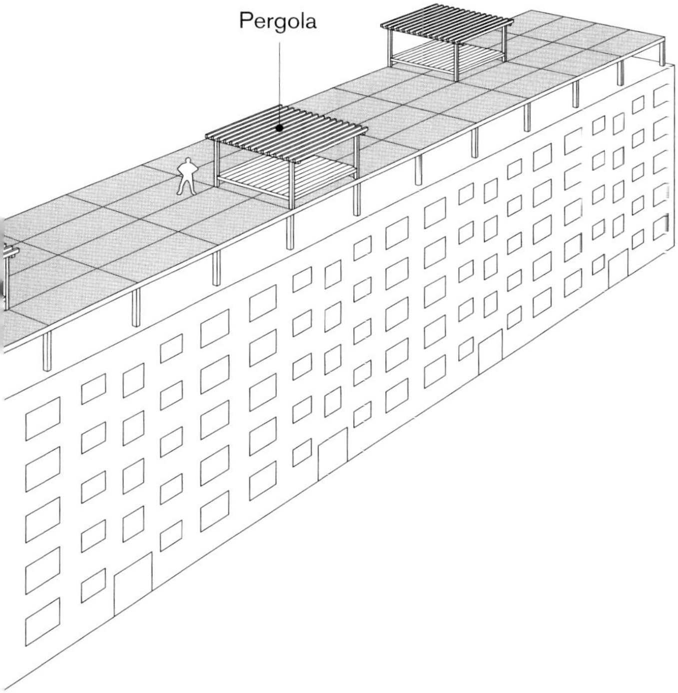
Pergola

014
Top Gard

Lightweight plastic is used to create an artificial deck for implementing a garden. Residents can use the roof as a semiprivate area. The peripheral area serves as a place for planting and as a handrail.

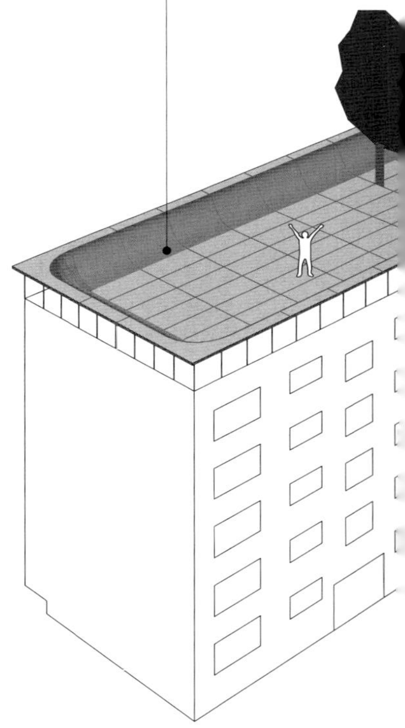

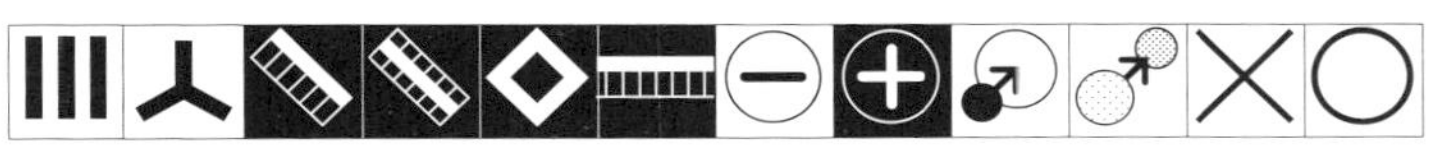

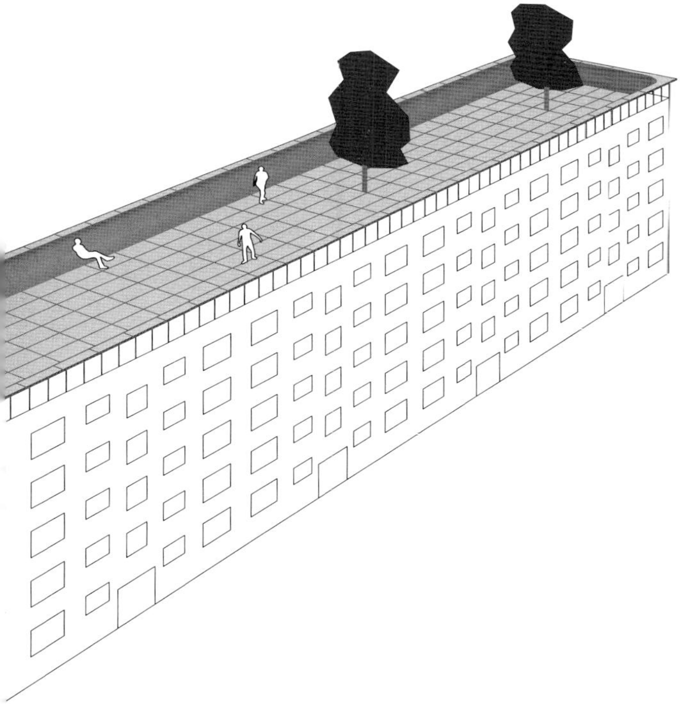

015
Top Con

The danchi's apartments are rather small and lack sufficient storage space. Thus, there is an overflow of objects in each dwelling. A megaframe is installed on the roof of a housing unit. Containers that serve as private storage spaces are positioned against this frame, which also supports access and steel staircases.

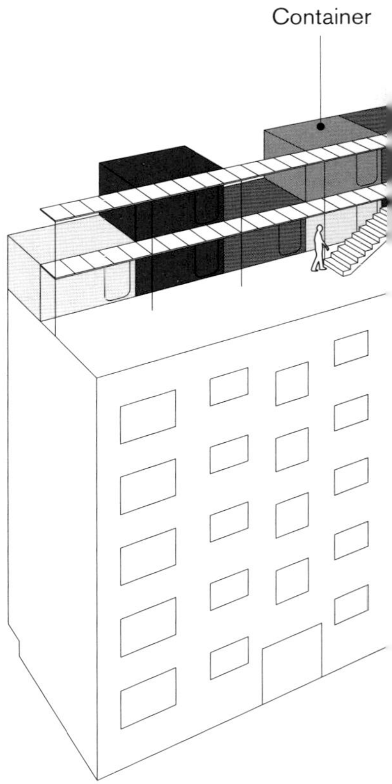

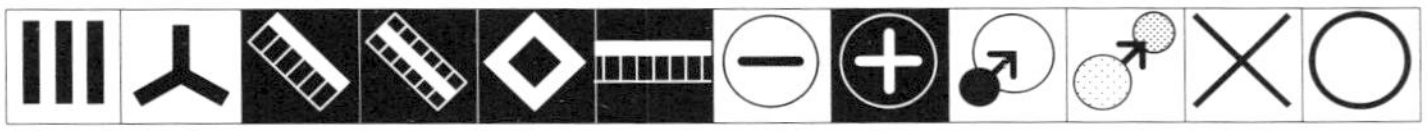

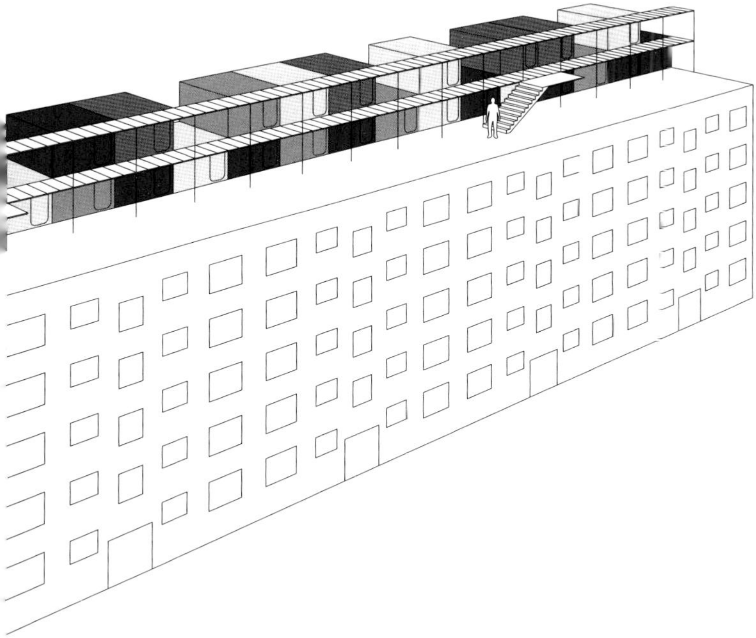

016
Rain House

Systems for collecting rainwater are increasingly being used as a result of interest in the environment. The large surfaces of the danchi's flat roofs are perfect for installing such a system. Rainwater is first collected on the roof surface, then directed to a primary tank. A series of smaller secondary tanks are set up in the gardens. Each user can open a valve and pump water when needed.

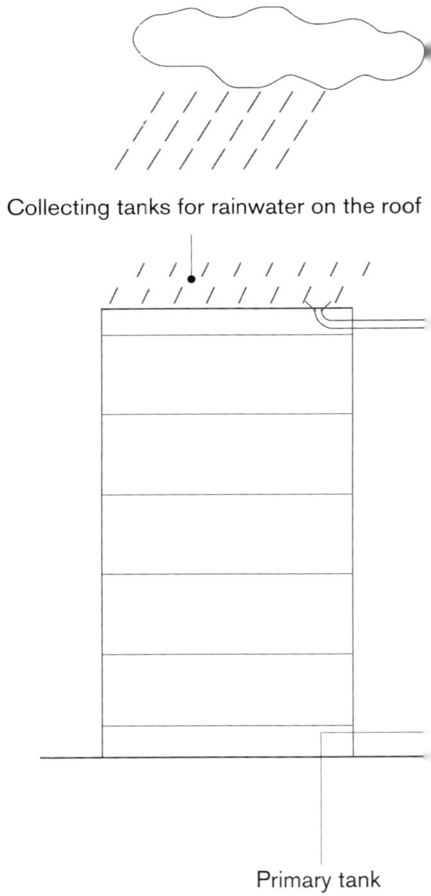

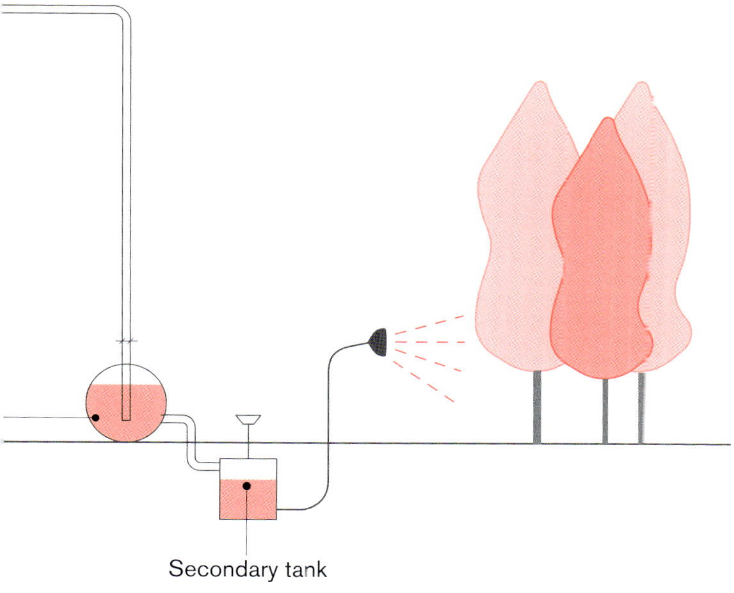
Secondary tank

017 Top Mesh

A light structure made of a steel mesh is fixed to the roof and supports various everyday functions. Drying clothes, practicing golf, gardening, or nursery school are some of the activities and hobbies that can take place under the net.

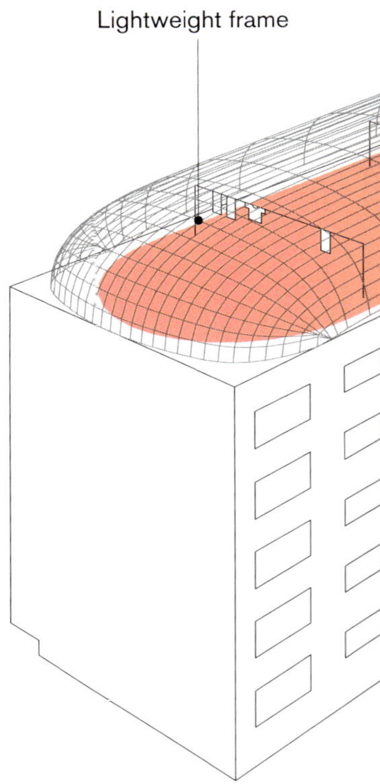

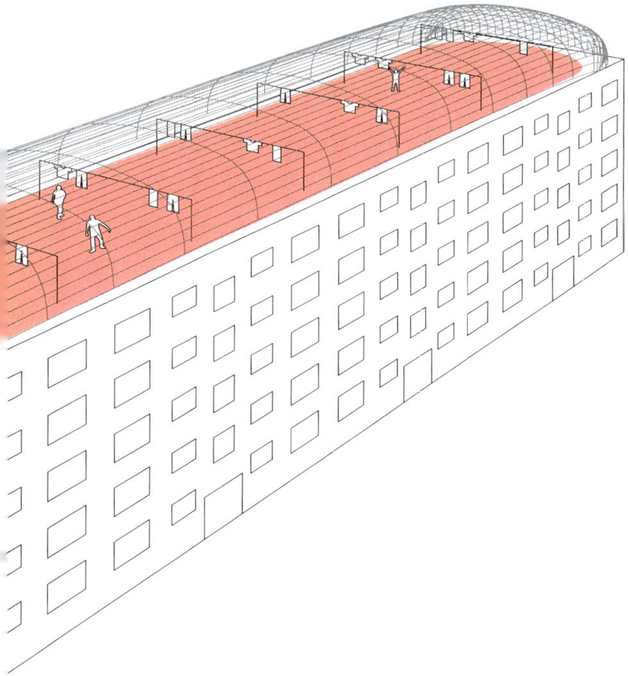

018
Top Res

A glass curtain wall fixed on the exterior of the building serves as a decorative surface and creates a space that can be used for commercial purposes. The drawing portrays a restaurant. Until now, commercial spaces have been absent from danchi estates, but such a change addresses the evolution of lifestyles and the aging population.

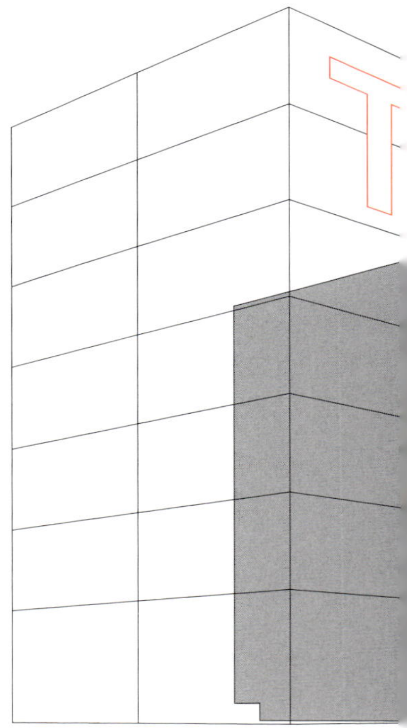

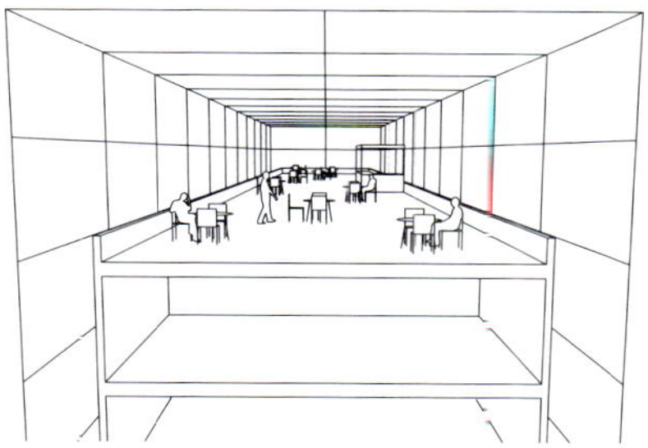

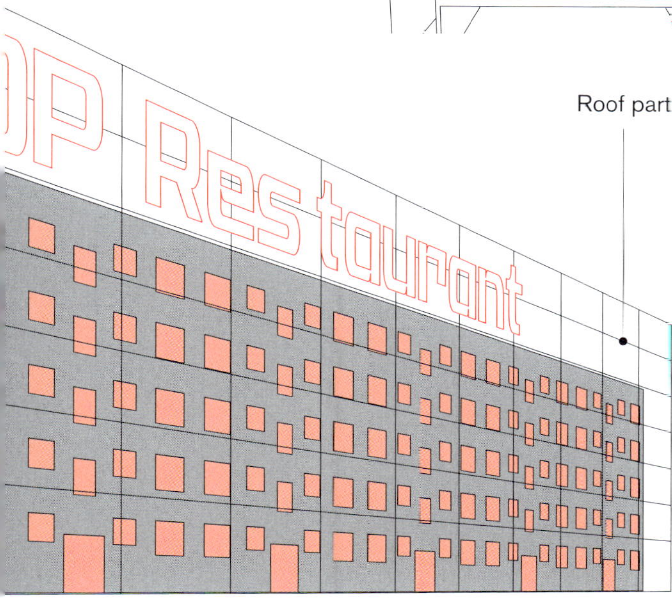
Restaurant
Roof part

019 Bill Buil

Sources of information like billboards constitute a main element of cityscapes. People living in city centers with commercial ads on their buildings accept this situation positively and handle the downside of living in such expensive and annoying environments by setting the switch-off time for ads. The outer walls of housing units used as commercial signboards can be coordinated by a simple systematization of their components such as plain surfaces, fences, and openings.

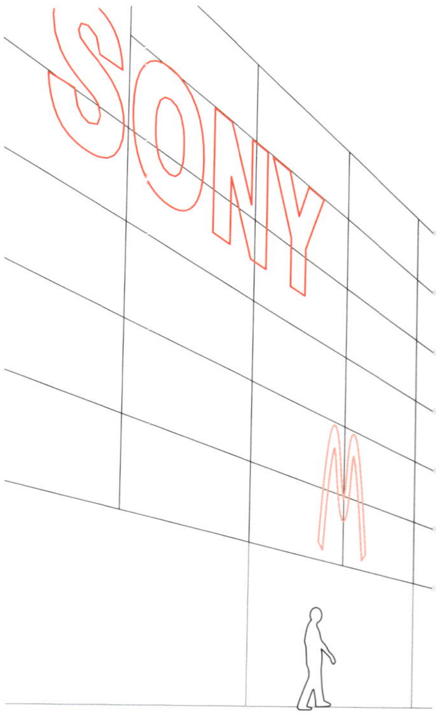

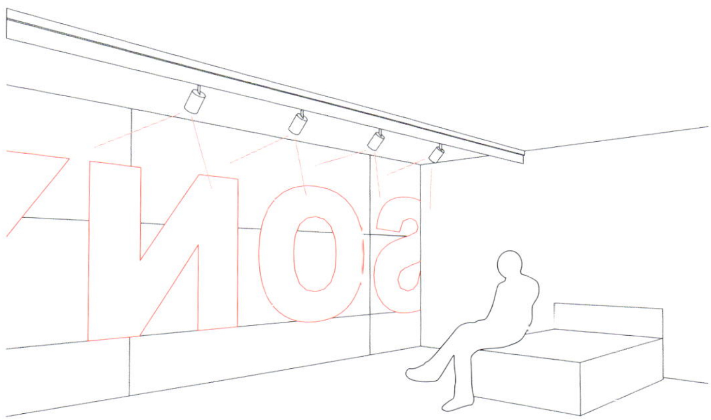

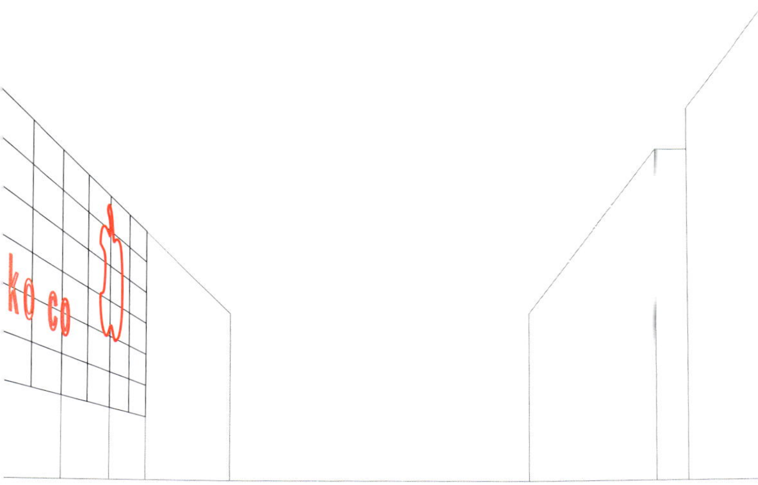

020 Botanical Face

To face the difficult challenge of providing a sufficient green coverage ratio in danchi located in highly urbanized areas, various devices are necessary. A green planting system on the outer wall helps to reduce the amount of sunshine and is effective in terms of insulation. Casting light concrete on existing walls and spraying plant seeds on the new surface is one solution. Another one is to fix mesh and planter boxes.

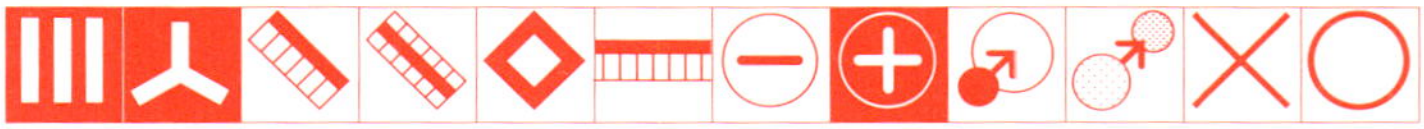

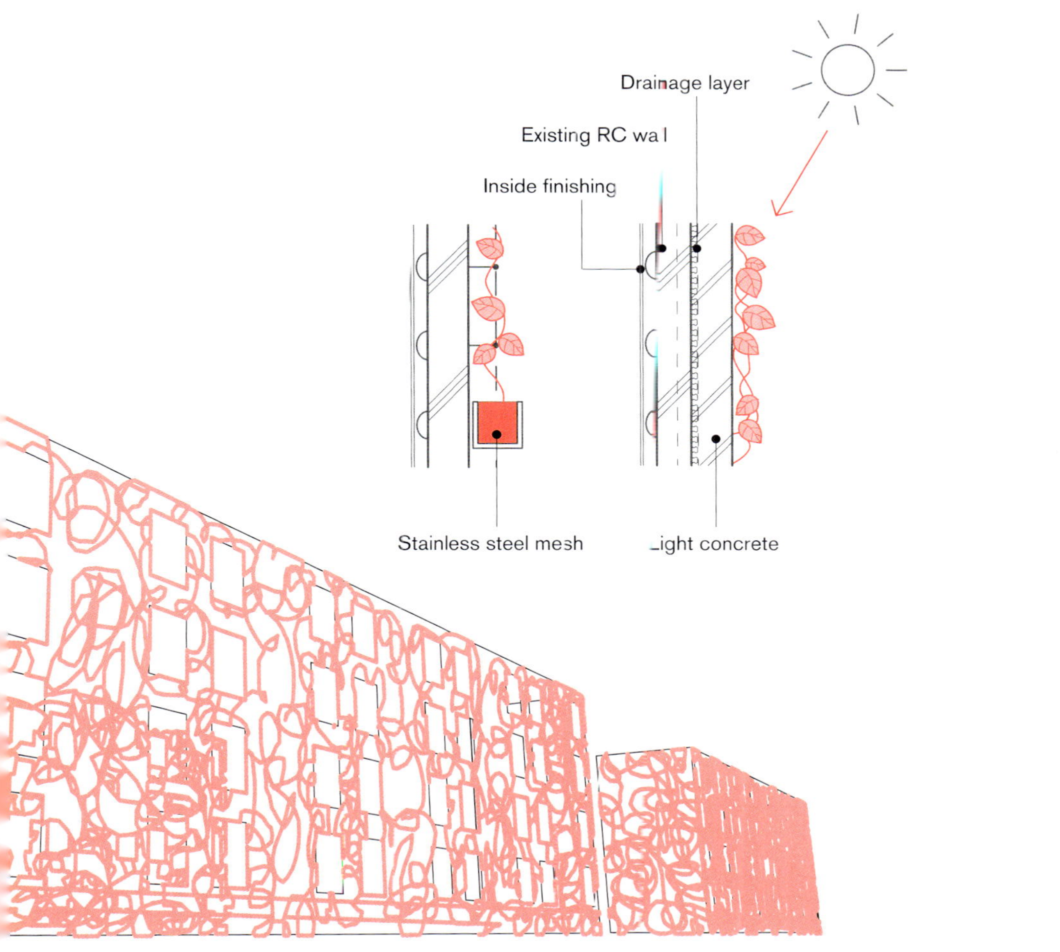
Drainage layer
Existing RC wall
Inside finishing
Stainless steel mesh
Light concrete

021
Sun Sun Sun

A set of solar panels used for converting light energy into electricity is added to housing units. The panels are fixed on the roof and on the terrace of each building. The maintenance work and adjustment of the solar panels' direction are left to the inhabitants. A portion of the electricity is used by residents, and the rest is sold to the electric power company. The panels display various colors recalling a set of electric futons (traditional Japanese bed blankets), like the ones housewives used to put out to dry on their terraces.

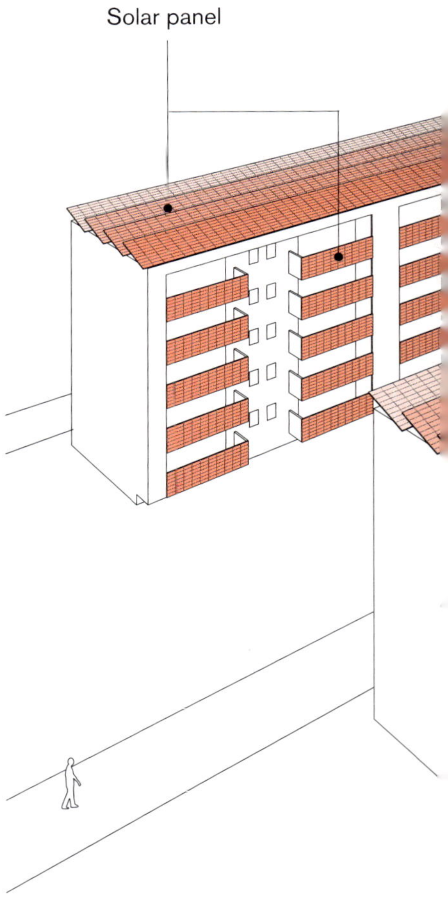

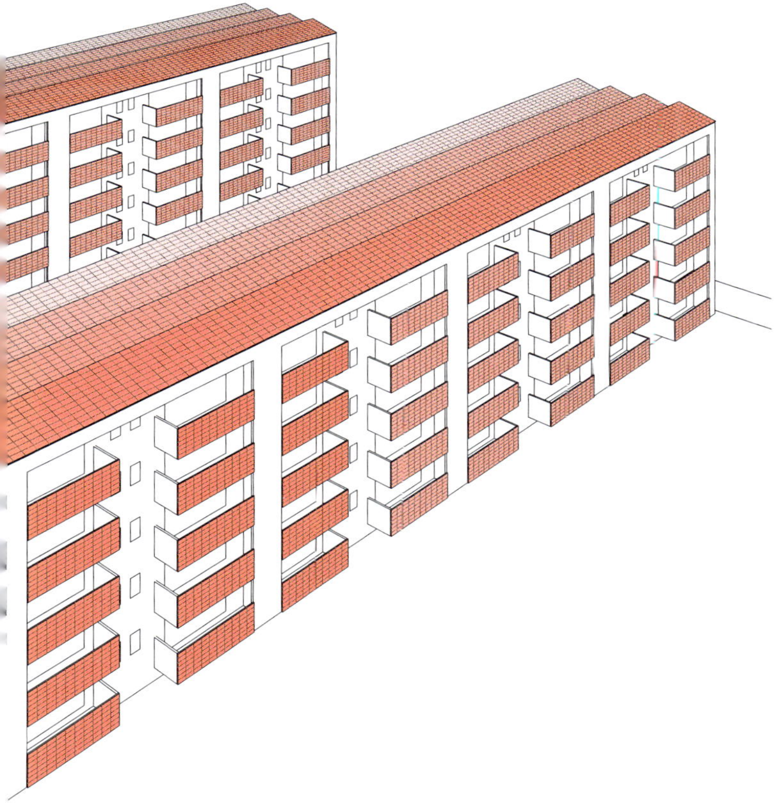

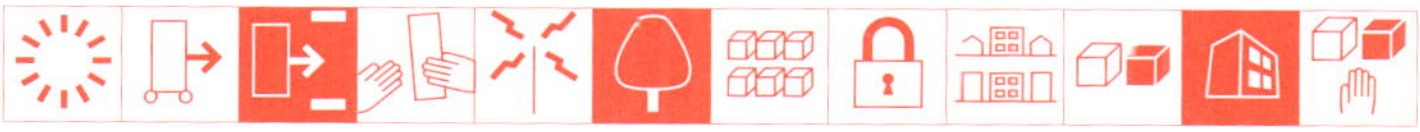

022 Taishin Finishing

Seismic reinforcement (taishin) is indispensable for housing units built from the mid-nineteen-fifties until the nineteen-seventies. However, reinforcement by means of braces is neither aesthetically pleasing nor easy to adapt for other purposes. Therefore, a reinforcement method that changes the outer wall of the building is implemented.

Poured on site RC finishing
Reinforcement with RC poured on site with reusable plastic molding panels provides a variety of expressions

Carbon fiber finishing
Reinforcement with carbon fiber and a finishing of epoxy resin shows the unique aspect of a black cloth with a shiny surface

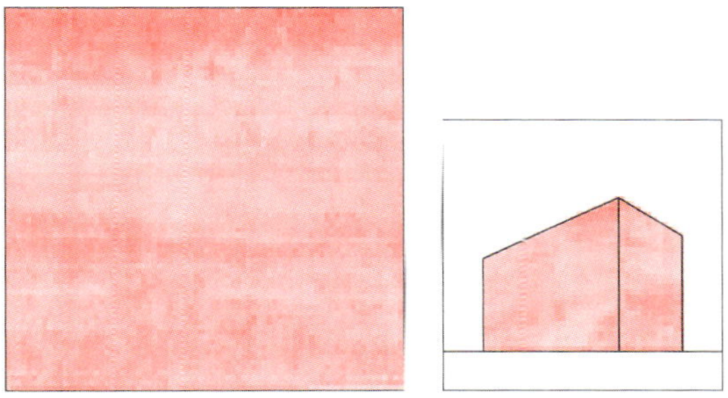

Poured on site RC finishing

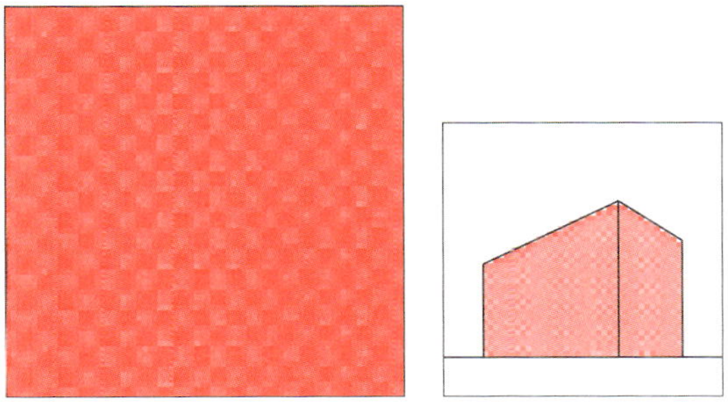

Carbon fiber finishing

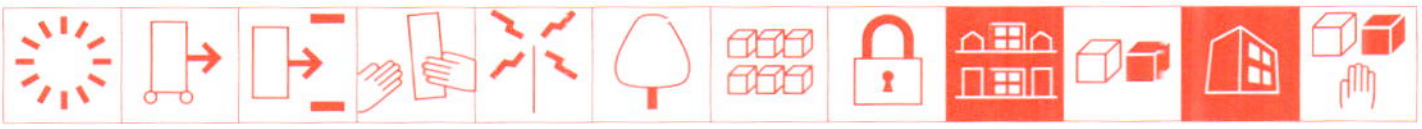

023 Cheese

Made of fleshy, translucent, high-grade plastic—which is earthquake resistant and fireproof—this system covers the exterior walls as seismic reinforcement. By perforating the surface of the plastic, it can be used as an antiseismic brace.

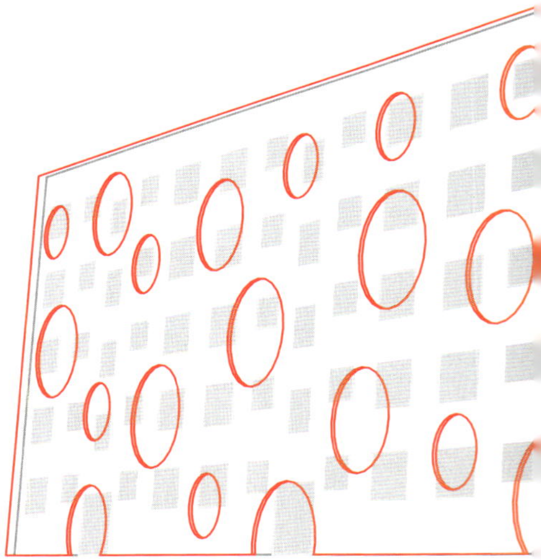

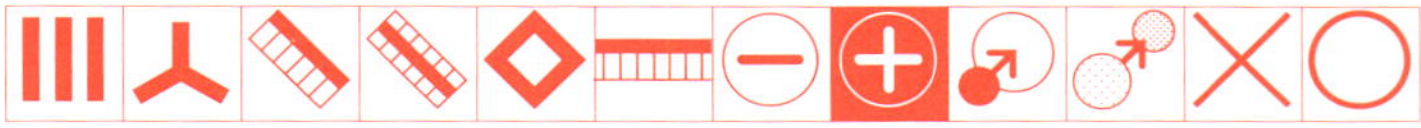

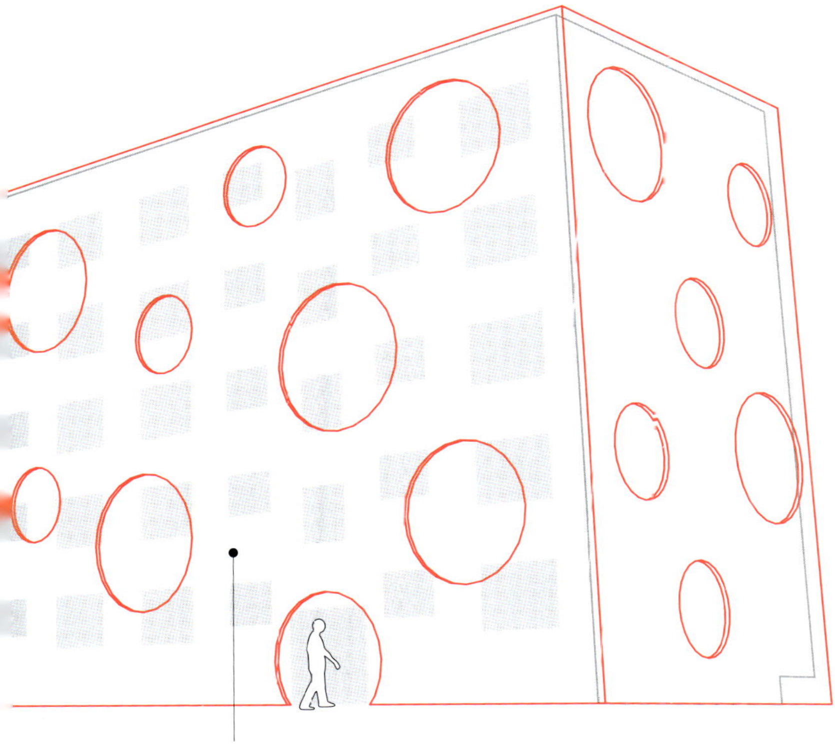

Cover

- Translucent fireproof wall made of thick plastic
- Perforated earthquake proofing brace

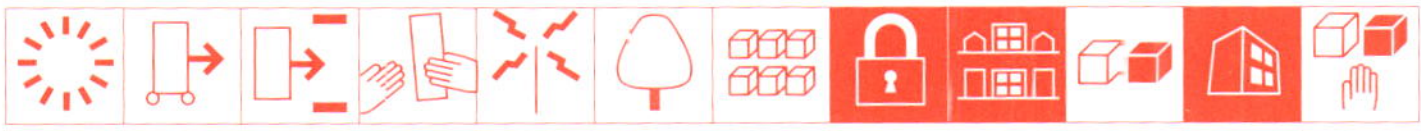

024
Art Wall

Side walls of housing units are usually simple, bare surfaces without windows. Here, the wall is offered to an artist as a place of expression. The tasteless scenery of conventional danchi becomes a gorgeous open-air gallery where different people will enjoy gathering.

Walls used as a canvas for artists

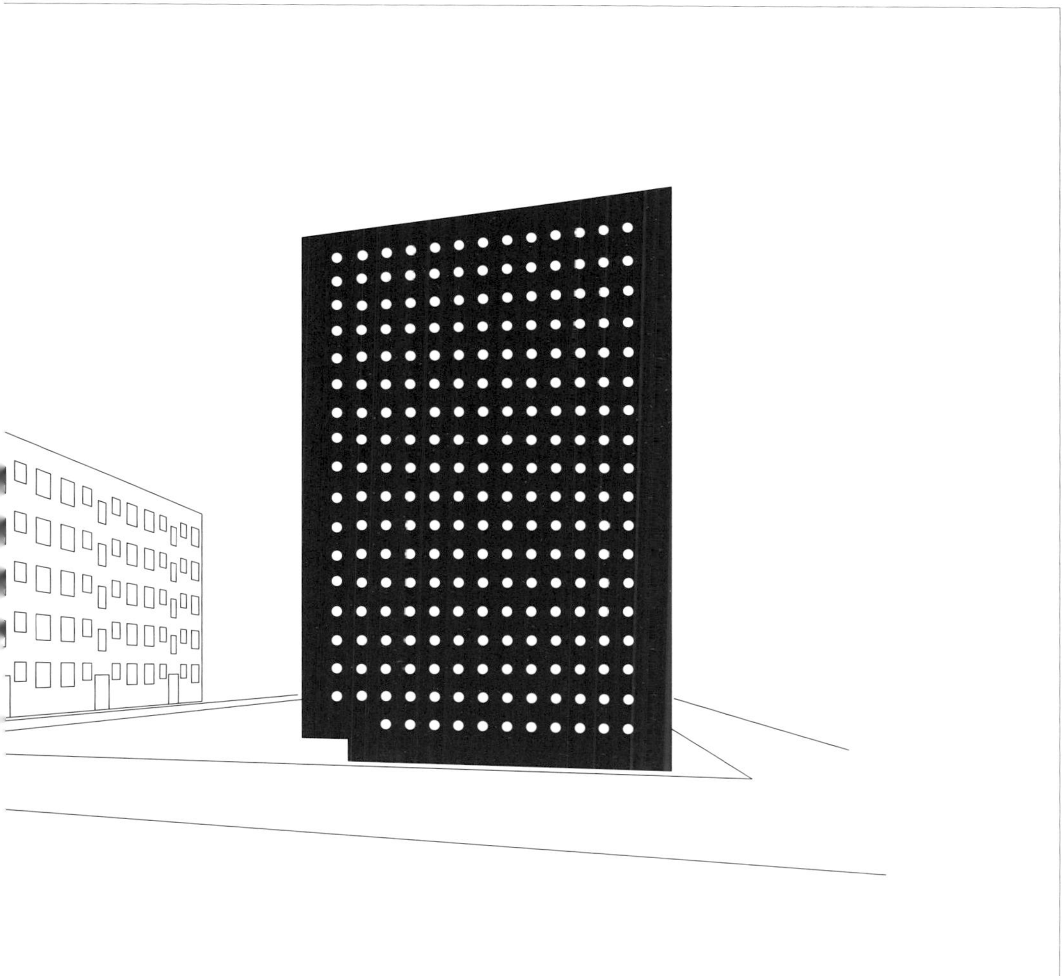

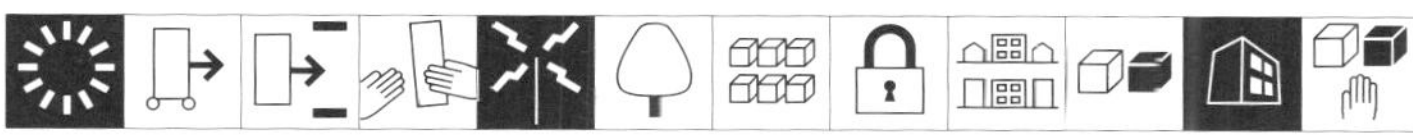

025
Cinema Wall

The bare side walls of housing units provide local inhabitants with good projection surfaces for outdoor movie theaters. Quiet nights in the danchi provide the perfect setting for a movie theater that revitalizes the estate.

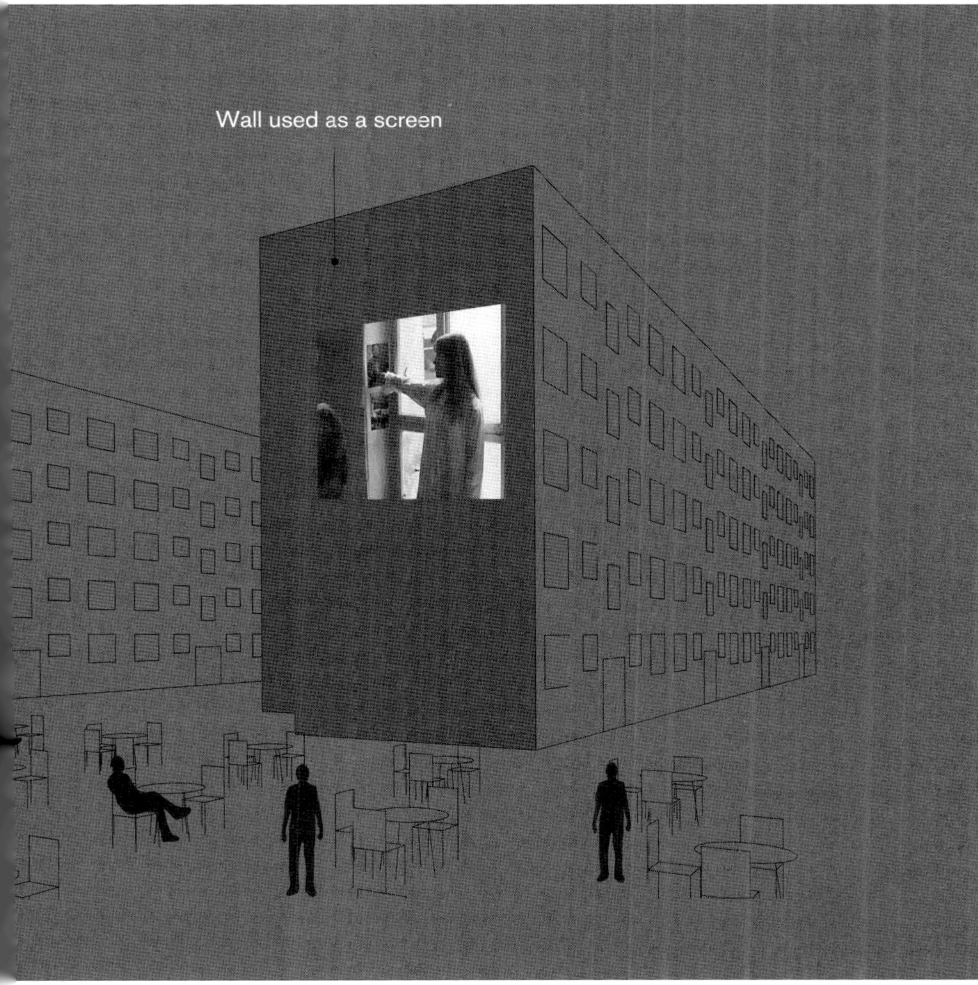
Wall used as a screen

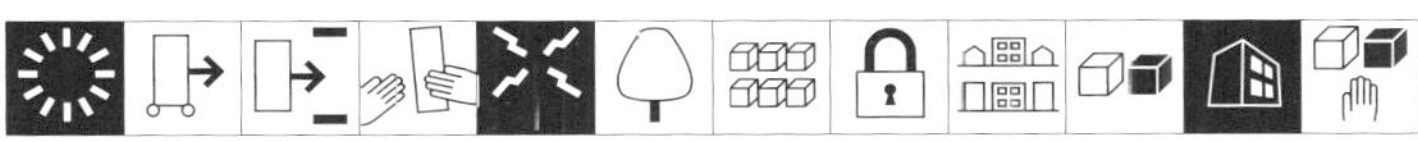

026
Eyes

Danchi have a few blind spots, which make criminal activity easier. A crime prevention system made from a glass screen with ceramic prints that show a series of eyes is implemented on the north side of a housing unit. The screen creates an atmosphere that helps to prevent crimes.

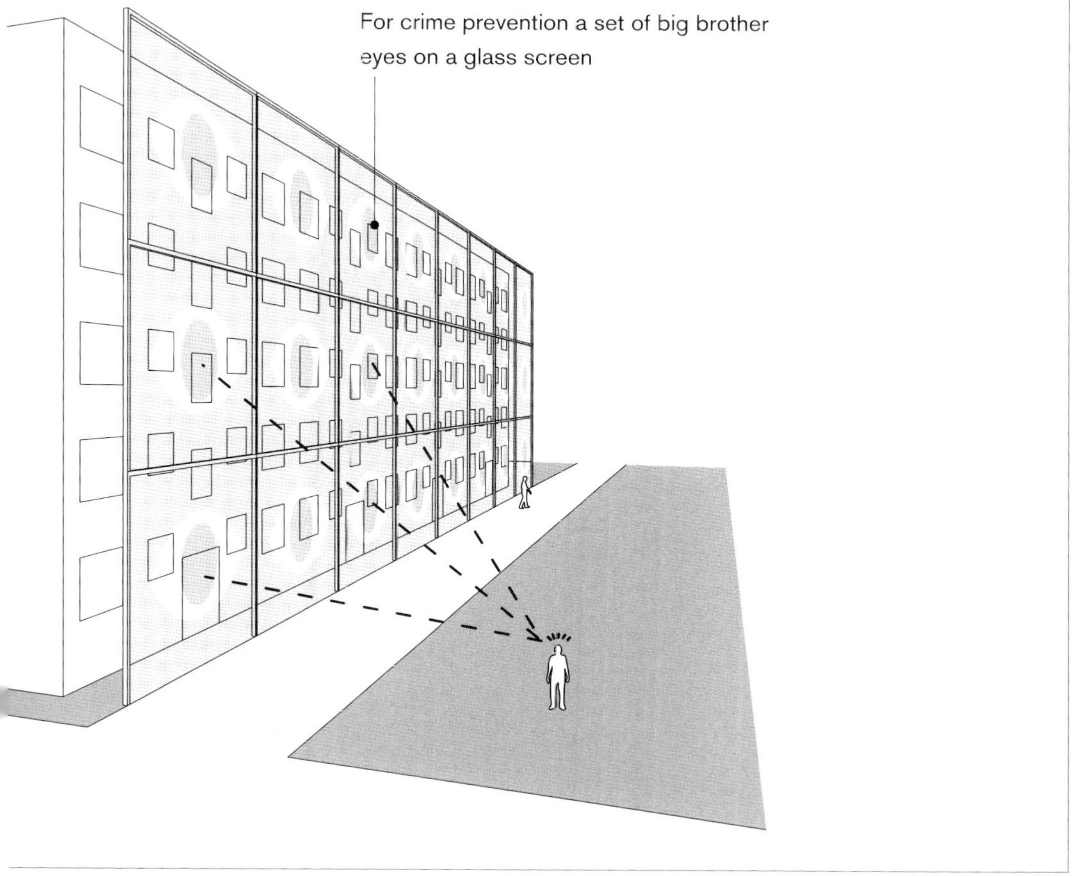
For crime prevention a set of big brother
eyes on a glass screen

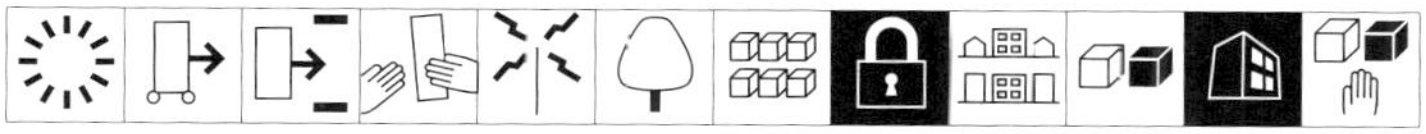

027
Cube

The outer wall of the housing unit is covered with semitransparent, high-strength plastic, which serves as a double skin. This device reinforces insulation performance and allows the use of solar energy, which is particularly effective in cold areas. In addition, the appearance of the existing housing unit's silhouette is revitalized.

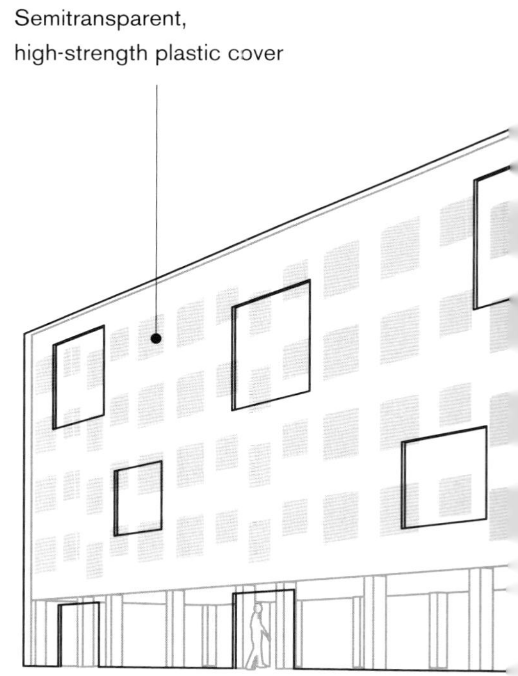

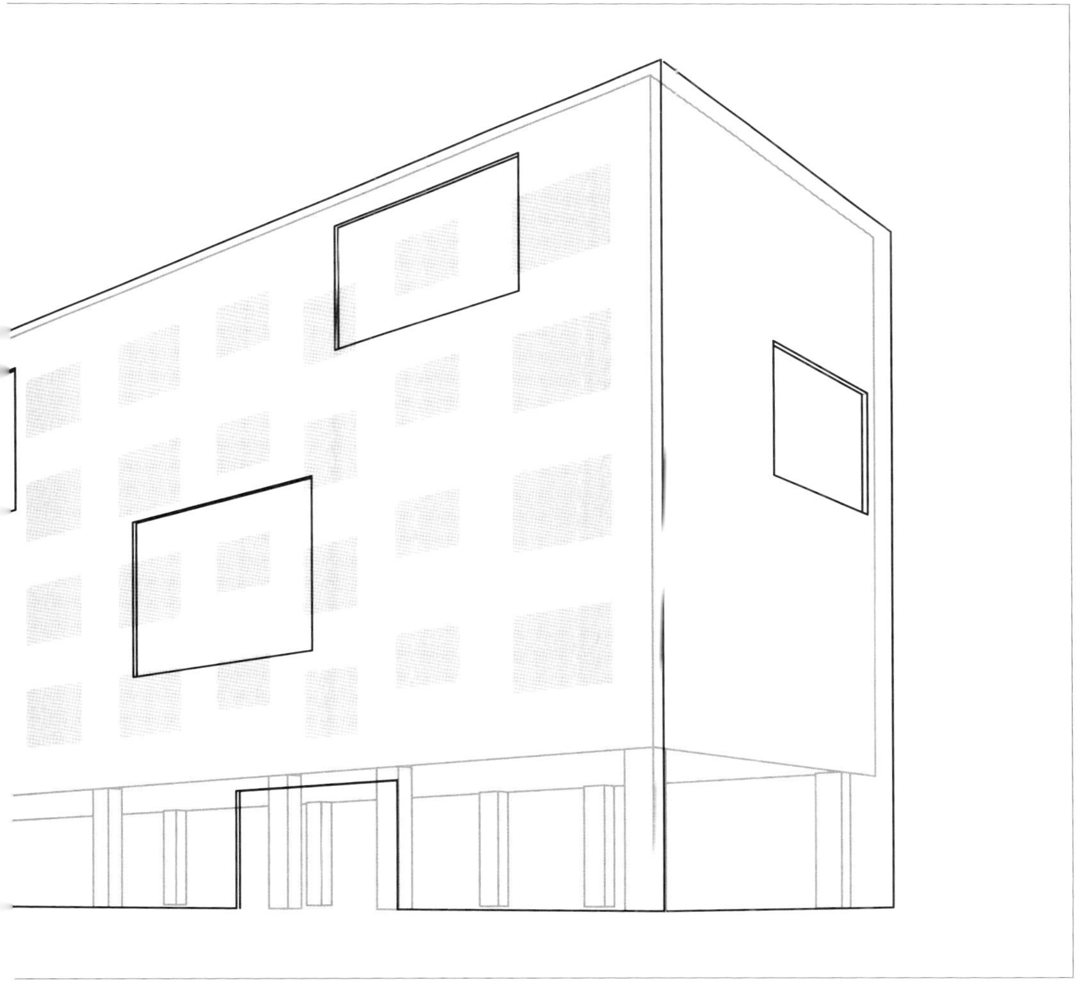

028
House Heat

The loss of energy due to air-conditioning typically installed in the existing housing units is high. One of the techniques used overseas for refurbishing multifamily housing is to add outer insulation to the existing façade. Its efficiency reduces the running costs of each apartment and helps to prevert global warming. This method also helps repair and renew the façades.

Insulation materials

Outer insulation system

Outer wall materials

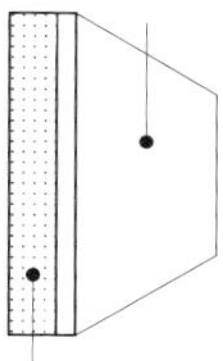

Several kinds of panels allow a variety of expressions

a. Hollow cement

b. ALC

c. Tiles

Polystyrene foam

Inner insulation system

Efficiency is lower than in outer insulation, though the construction is simple

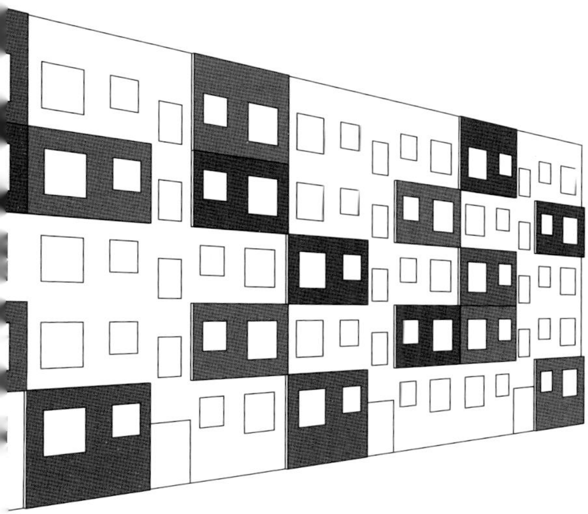

029 Exchange

A type of air pressure balloon roof system encloses the space between housing units.
The new space can be used for offices, machine rooms, and other facilities including concert halls, theaters, or gymnasiums.
Changing the use of the danchi's in-between spaces also revives the entire structure.

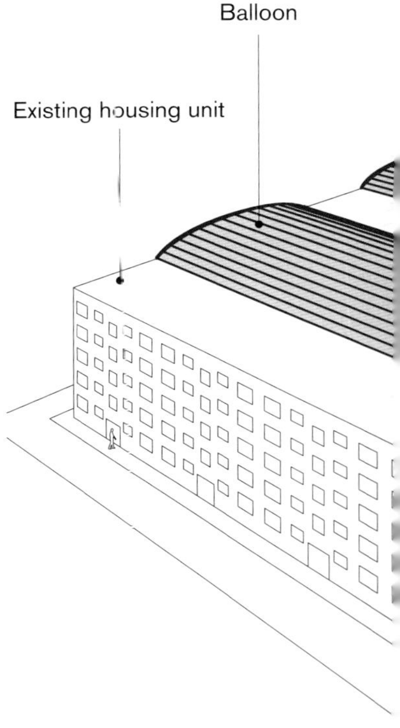

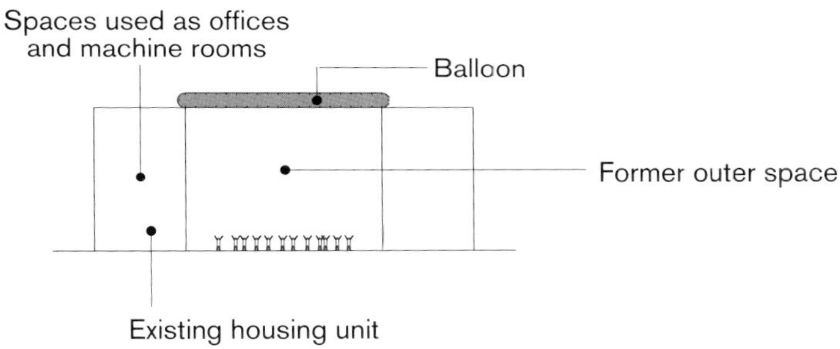
Spaces used as offices
and machine rooms
Balloon
Former outer space
Existing housing unit

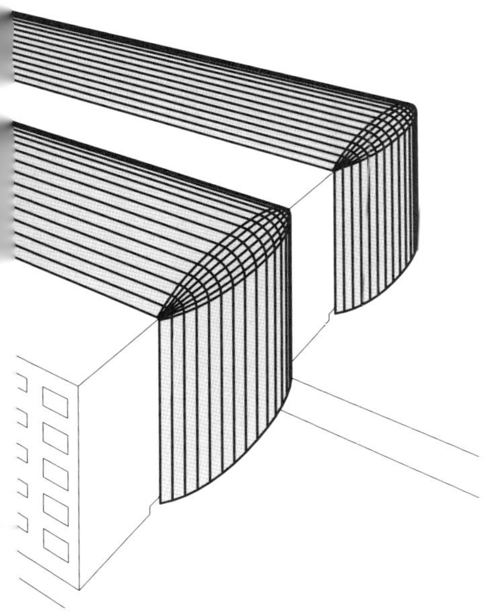

030
Short Cut

Activities within the housing units are separated because of the physical division of the buildings. Tying the units together with catwalks without having to access the ground floor will help solve this problem. Bridges with a truss structure either in steel or concrete are implemented by simply hollowing a single apartment and replacing it. Eventually, these bridges help reinforce the antiseismic structure. These catwalks can be used both as indoor and outdoor spaces where people hang their clothes out to dry or enjoy the coolness of the evening.

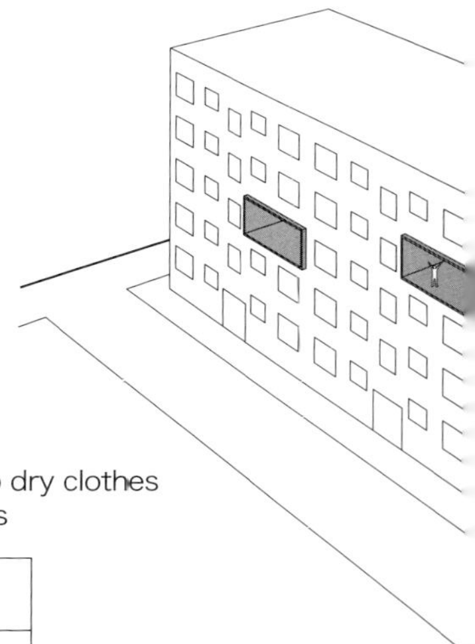

Passages and places to dry clothes and enjoy cool evenings

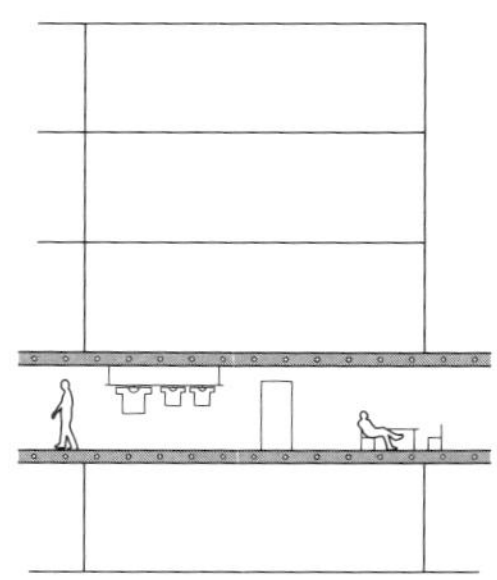

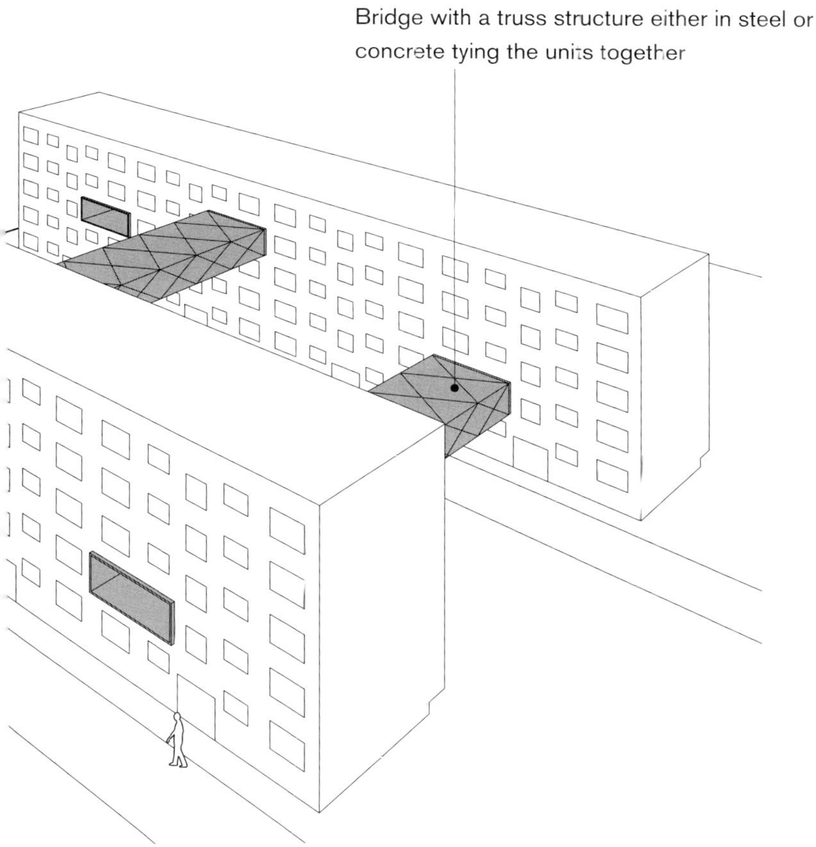
Bridge with a truss structure either in steel or concrete tying the units together

031
Market

The open space between the housing units is suitable for large gatherings. By covering this space with a mobile tent that can be opened and shut freely, events such as flea markets or large holiday gatherings can take place here.

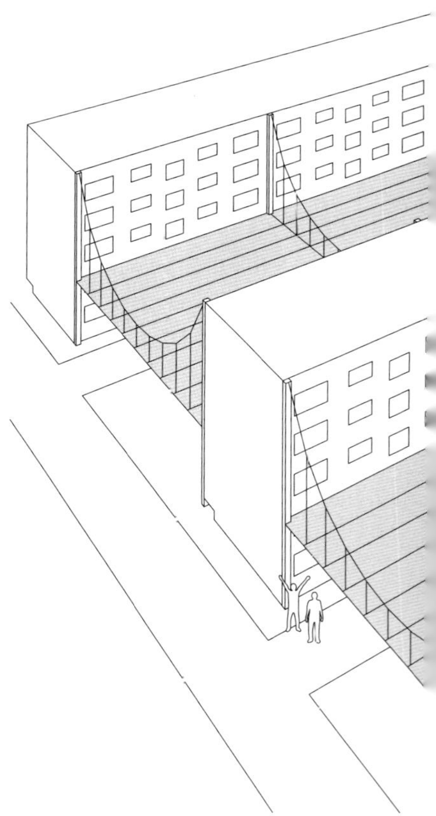

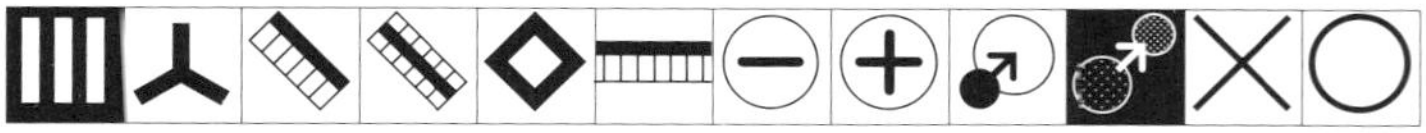

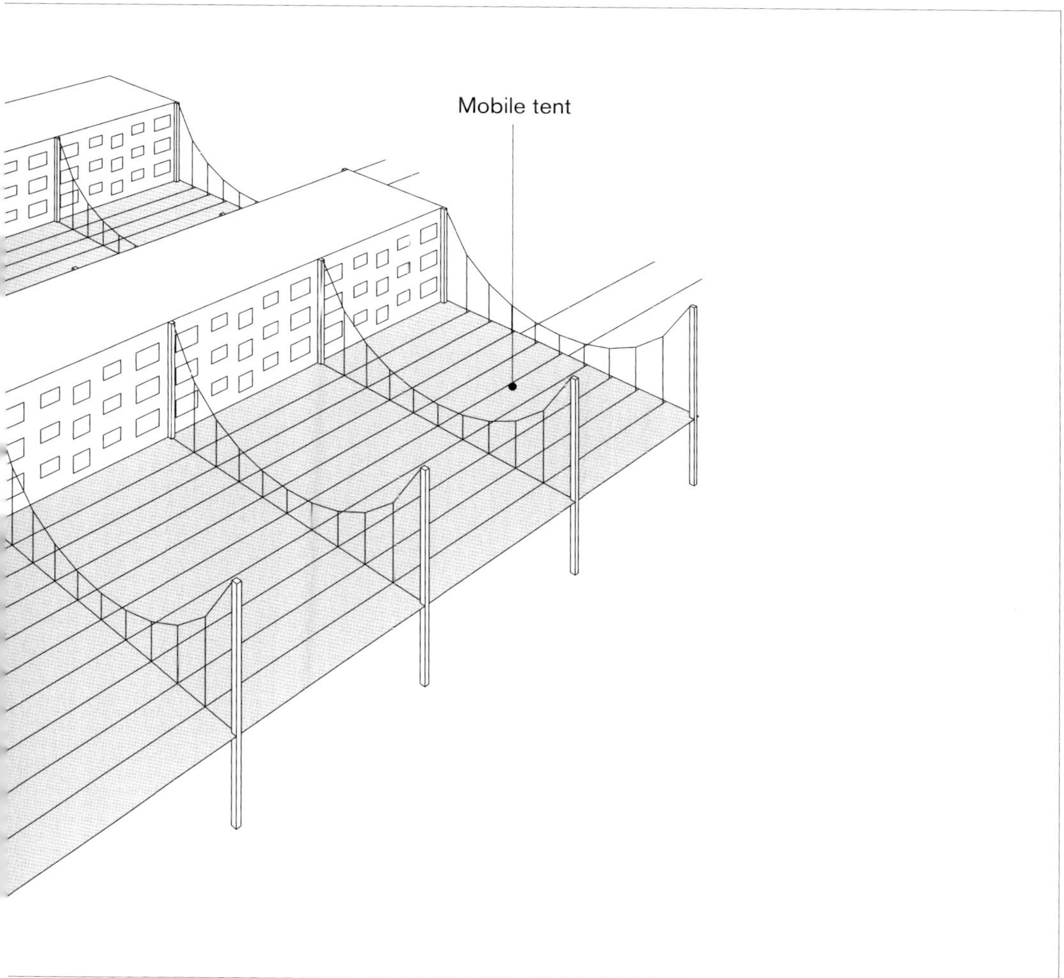
Mobile tent

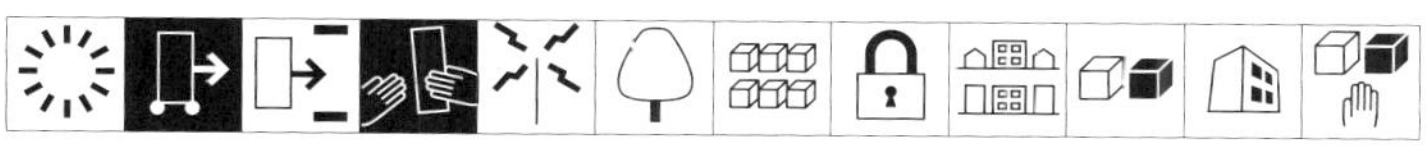

032
Hall in Hole

In order to reduce the feeling of oppression resulting from the huge slab-shaped appearance of the housing units, apertures are made through the building using unoccupied apartments. These holes bring light to the northern side of the housing units and also provide a room for gatherings and renewed contacts between the inhabitants.

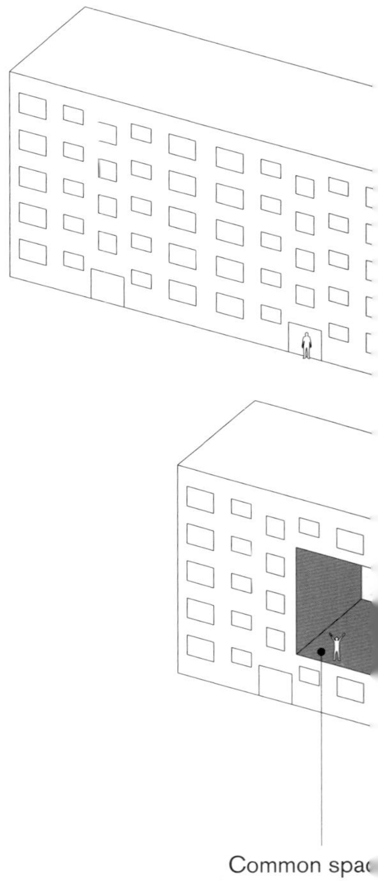

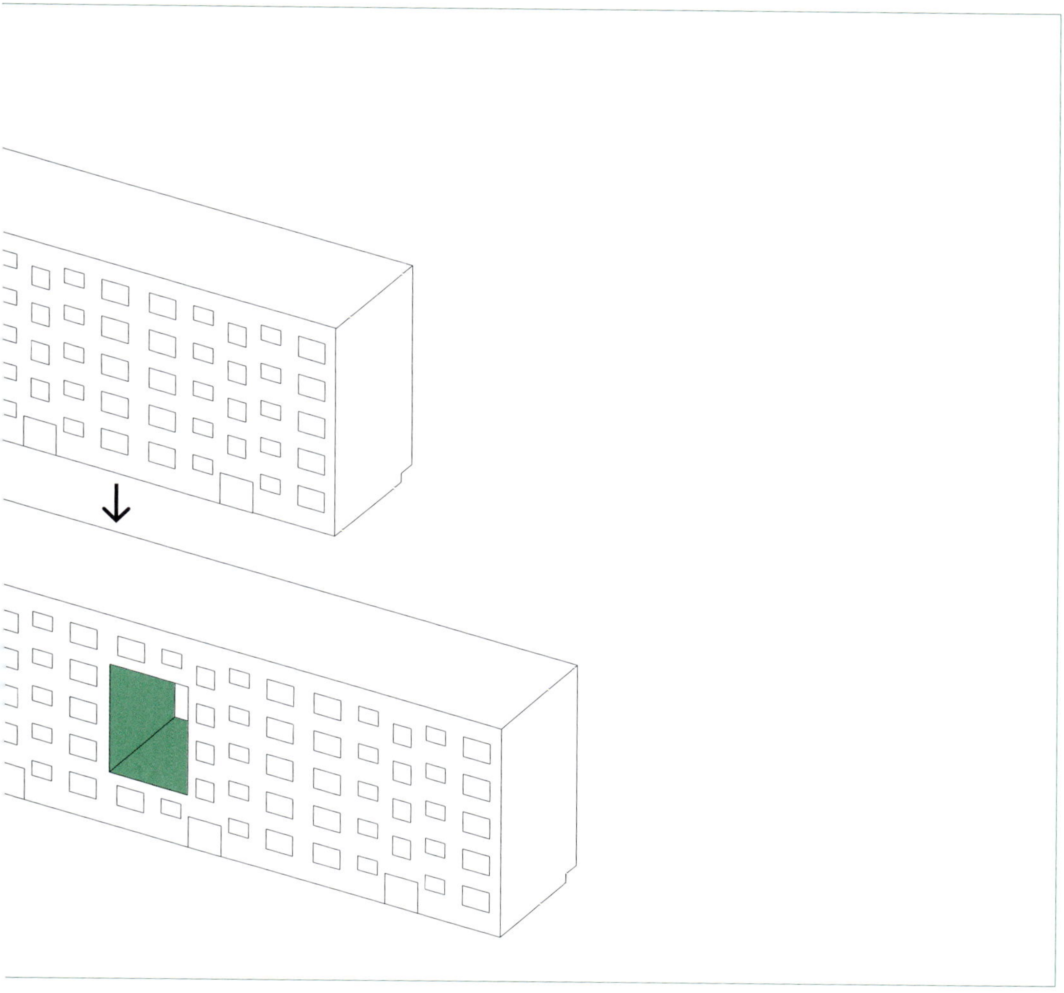

033
Air Park

The open space between the housing units, which is very green, is adapted for common use. Spaces between the trees are perfect for creating decks and open rooms, providing an oasis for residents.

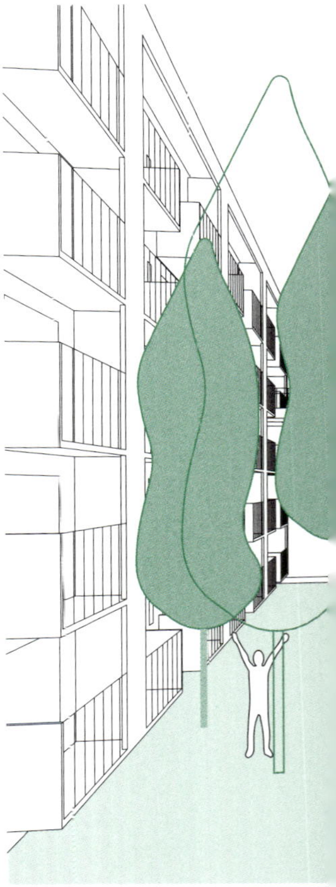

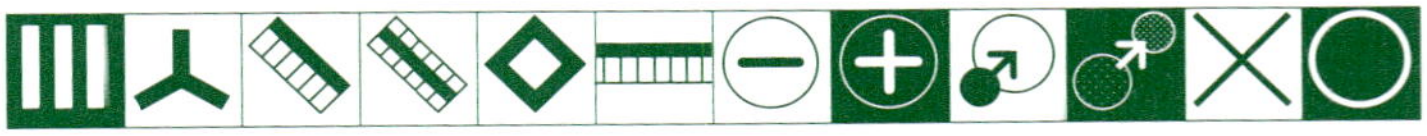

Recreation and relaxation space created
between the trees

034
Floating Room

The narrowness of the common space and the apartments in the danchi is problematic. An annex is built in the open space between the housing units, which helps to extend these surfaces. The outer volume becomes an inner one, though not touching existing trees. Because the annex is floating, it does not interfere with activities on the ground.

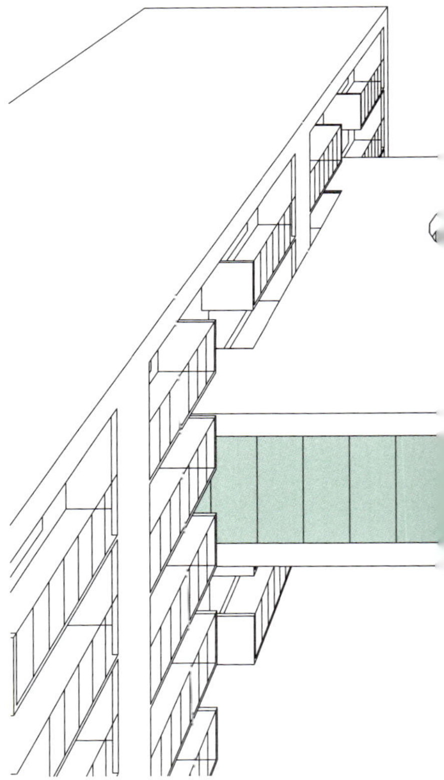

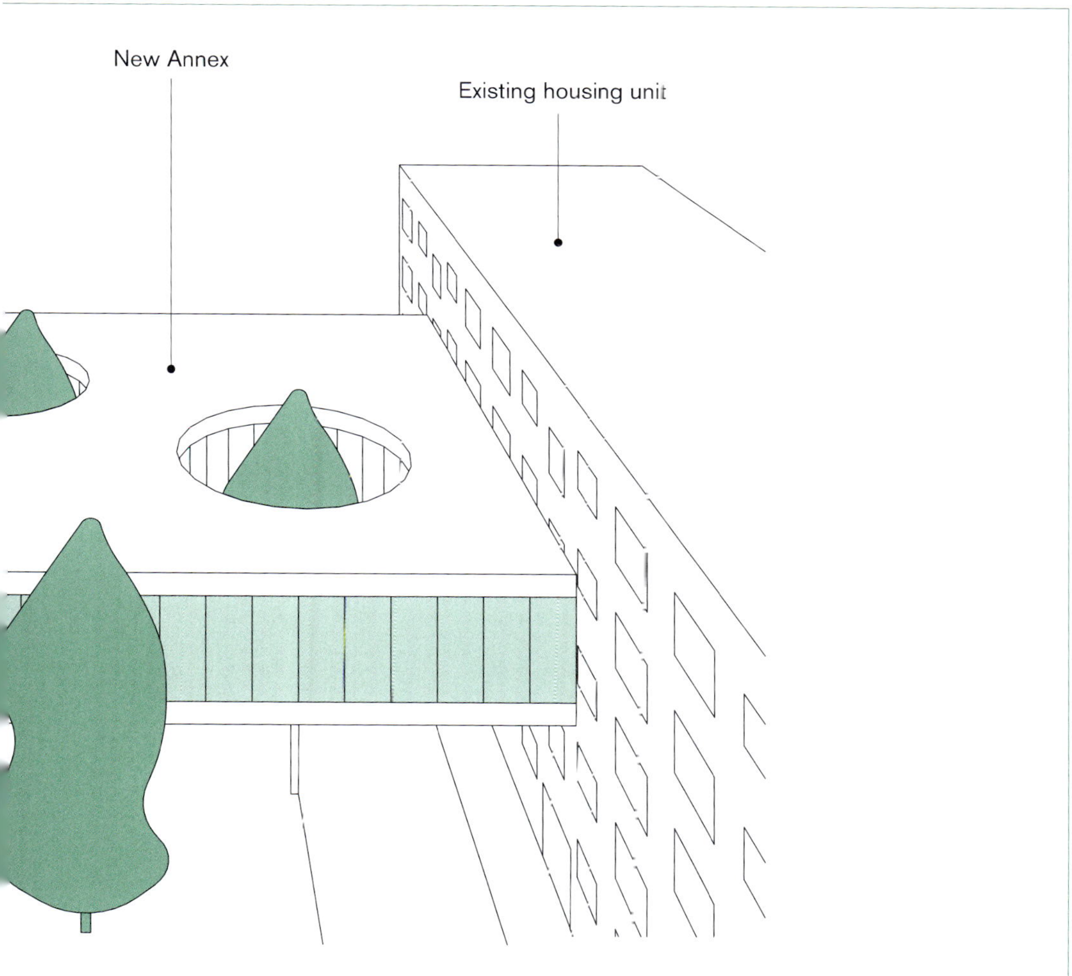
New Annex
Existing housing unit

035
Office Service

Danchi offer only a few minimum functions. A front desk system providing various services for residents in the densely inhabited housing units will be appreciated. In the entrance of every building, a front desk service similar to a hotel will respond to residents' requests for photocopies, faxes, cleaning, and home deliveries, etc.

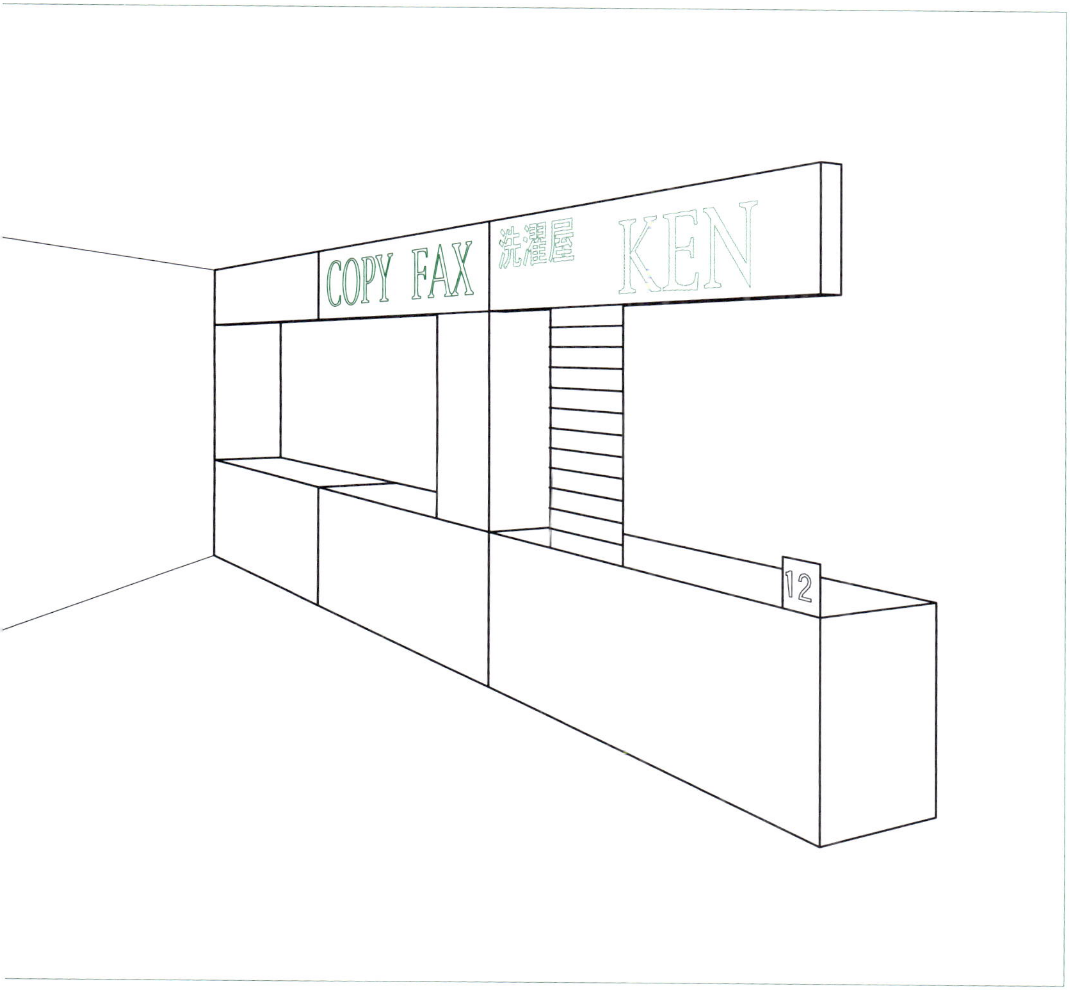
COPY FAX
洗濯屋
KEN
12

036
Stories of Balconies

Enlarging the half-landing platform of outdoor staircases will provide a useful place for breaks and communication for residents. Various options are proposed for covering the steel frame. Residents are free to select their preference.

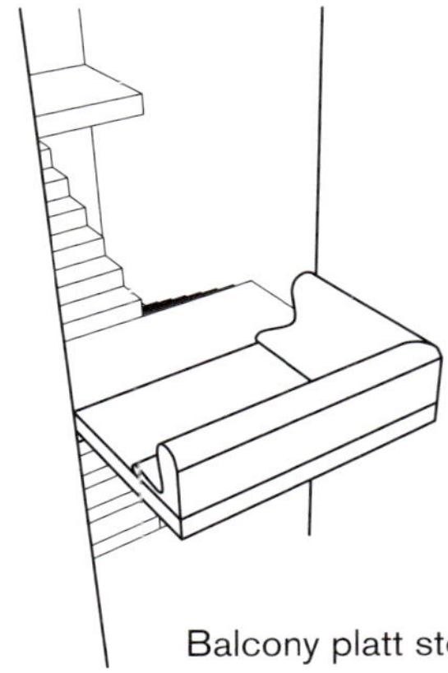

Balcony platt stop

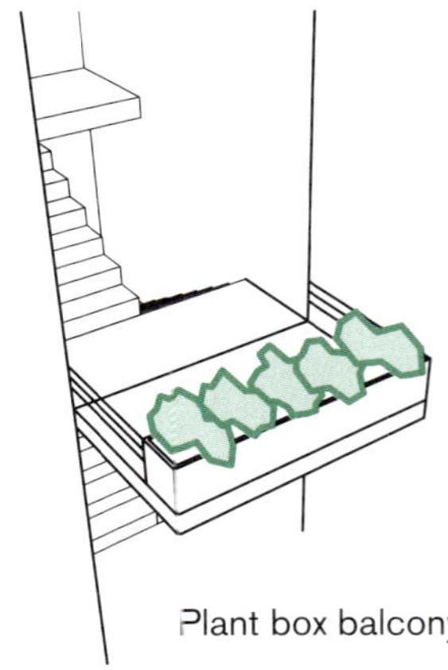

Plant box balcony

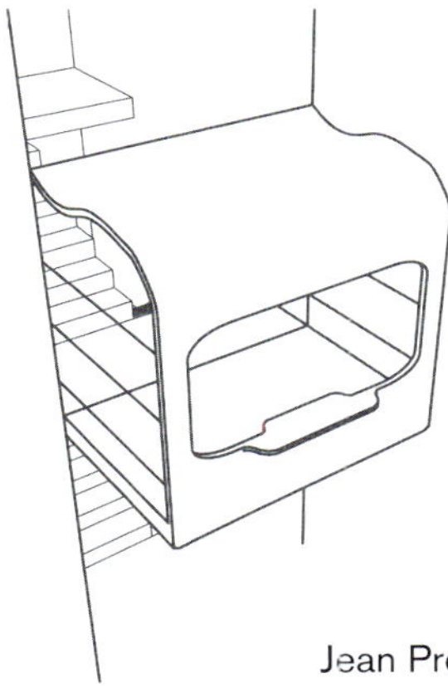

Jean Prouvé's balcony

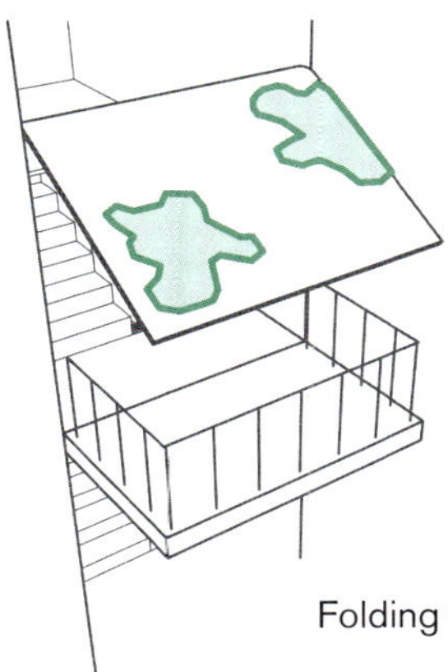

Folding tent balcony

037
Blooming in the Stairs

These are new staircase units that are installed outside after removal of the existing ones. They are covered with various kinds of materials. In this case, a metal mesh supports the green plants that make the open space resemble an alley of large trees.

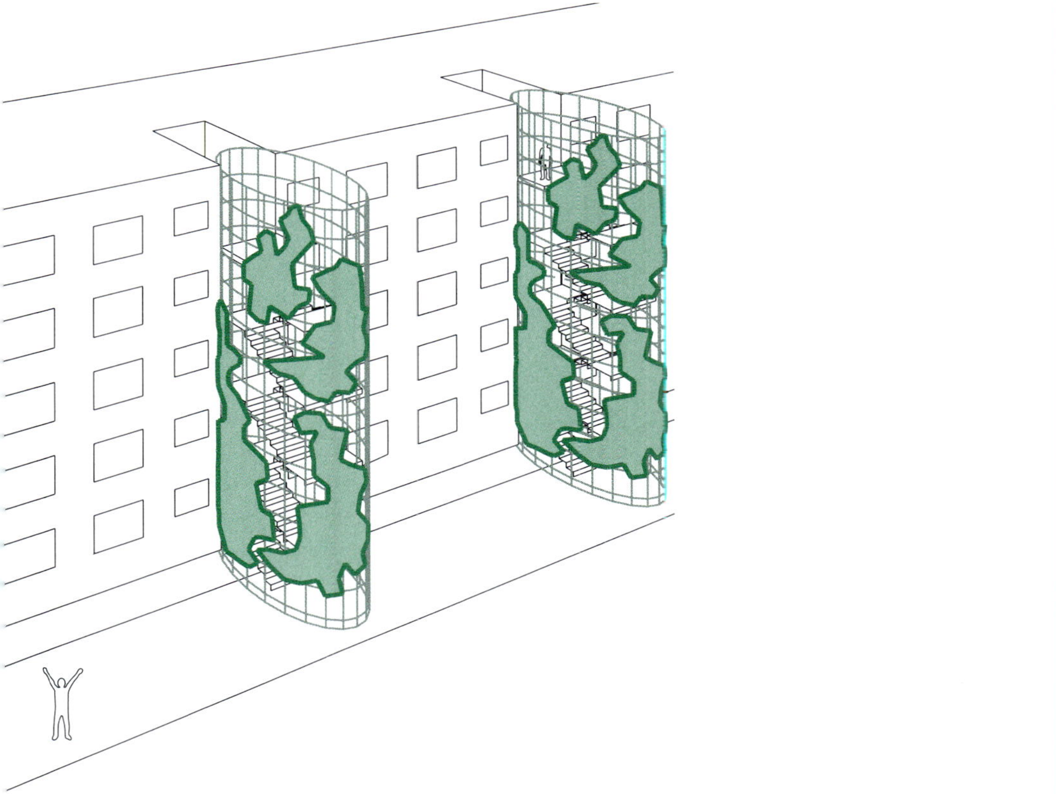

038
Cover Up

The entire staircase is covered with a metallic mesh that looks like a green wall continued by a pergola over the entrance. Entering the building and climbing the stairs becomes playful, especially when flowers and seasonal fruits are blooming.

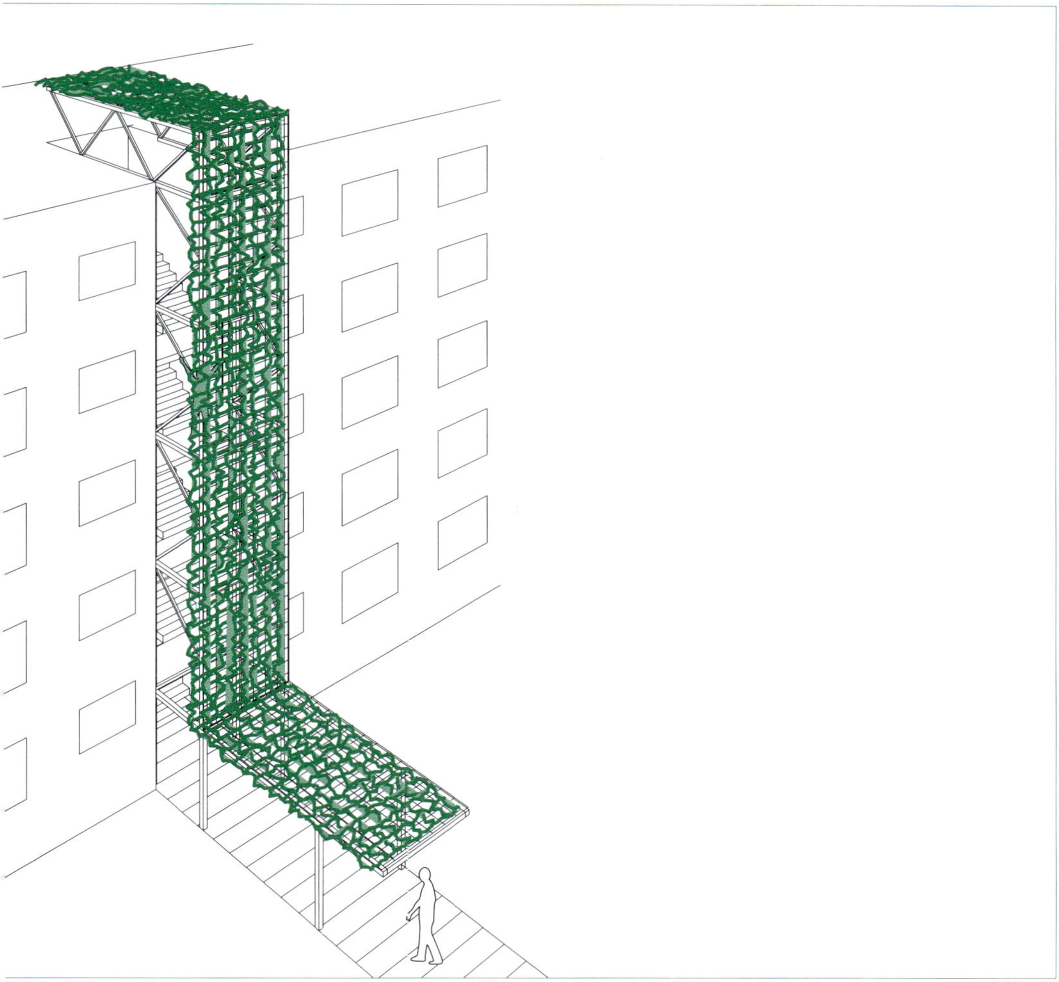

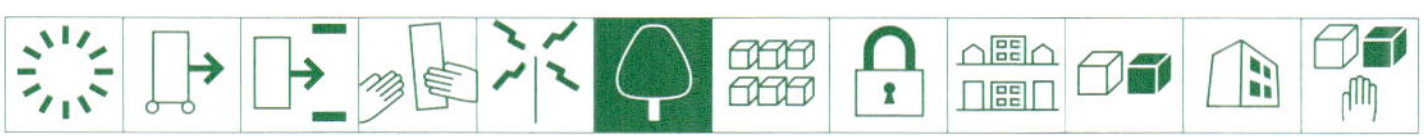

039
Stairs In, Stairs Out

A space that brings light inside the housing unit is provided by removing the stairs from their former location. Adding a long awaited elevator will make the way to each apartment easier and reinforce the privacy of entrance doors. It will also remove a structural burden from the existing housing unit.

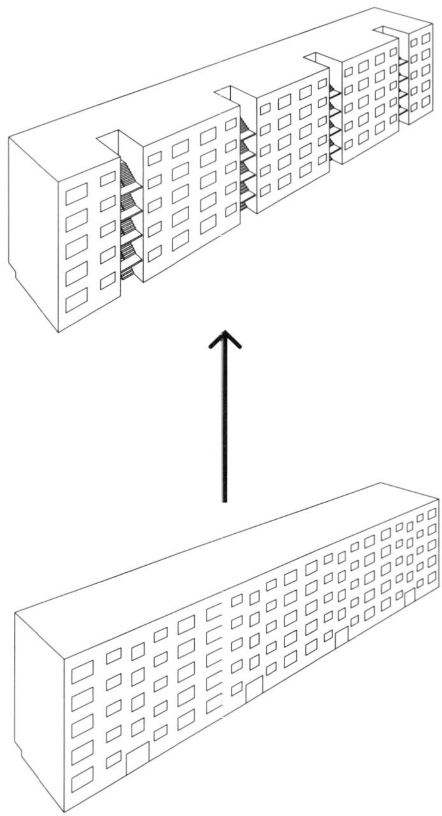

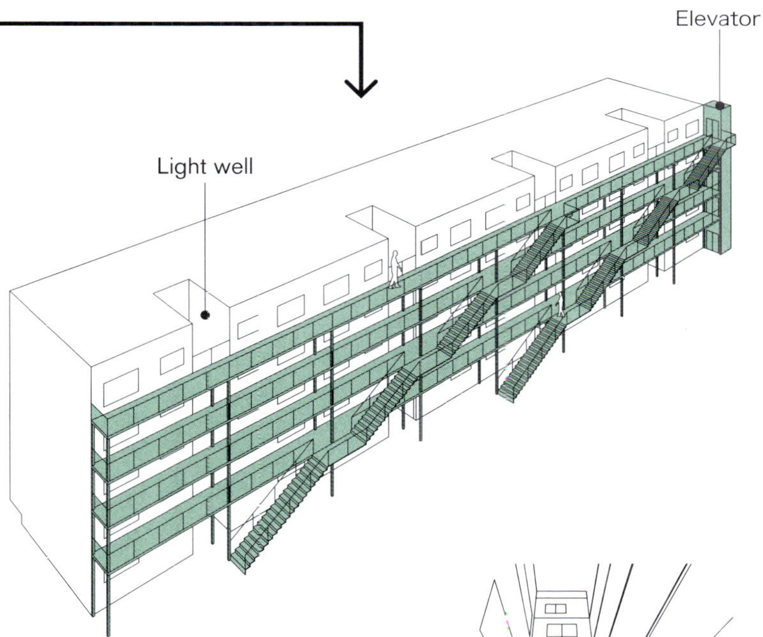
Elevator
Light well

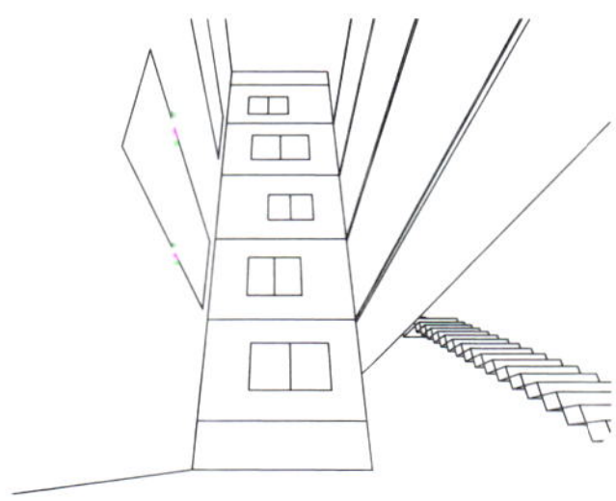

040
Ceiling Up

Reducing the number of floors of a housing unit will address the danchi apartments' typically low ceilings. Increasing the height of the wall will also be useful for adding benches, storage, and other devices.

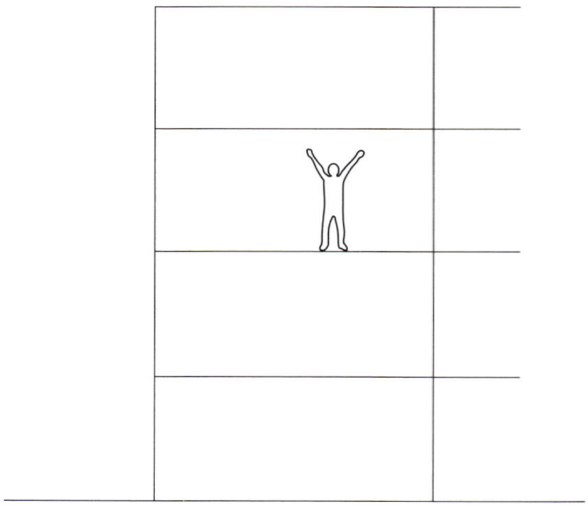

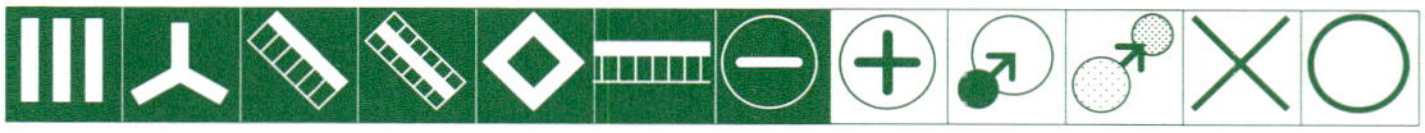

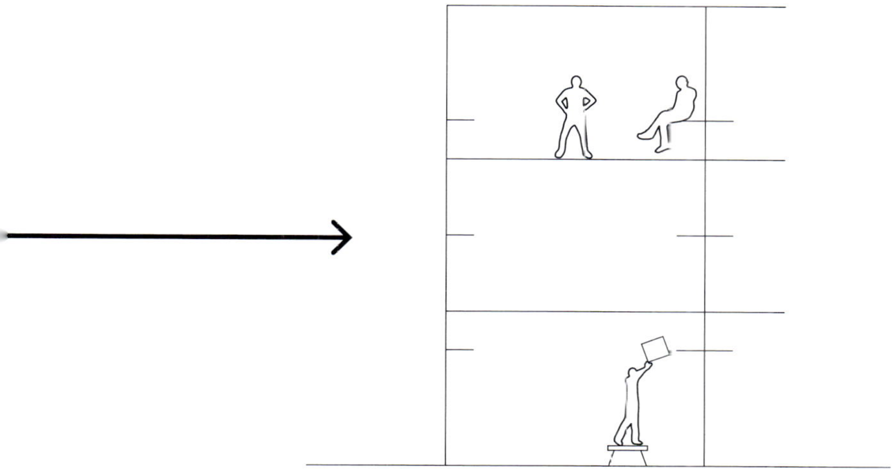

041 Co Bath

A bathhouse for collective use is implemented as a representative facility for the community living in the danchi. An empty apartment house is refurbished to host between ten to twenty residents, like the small public baths that still exist in the city.

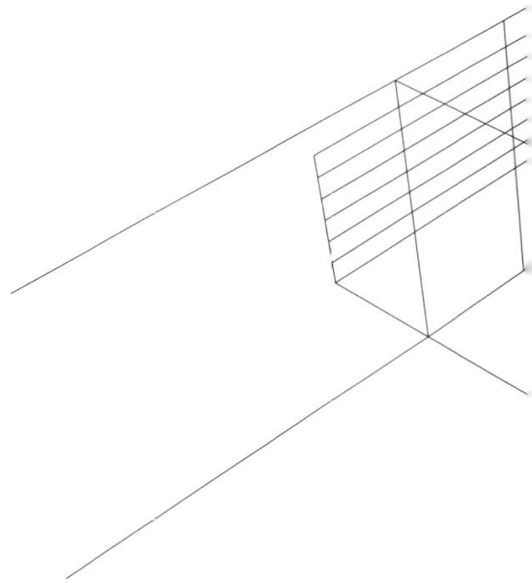

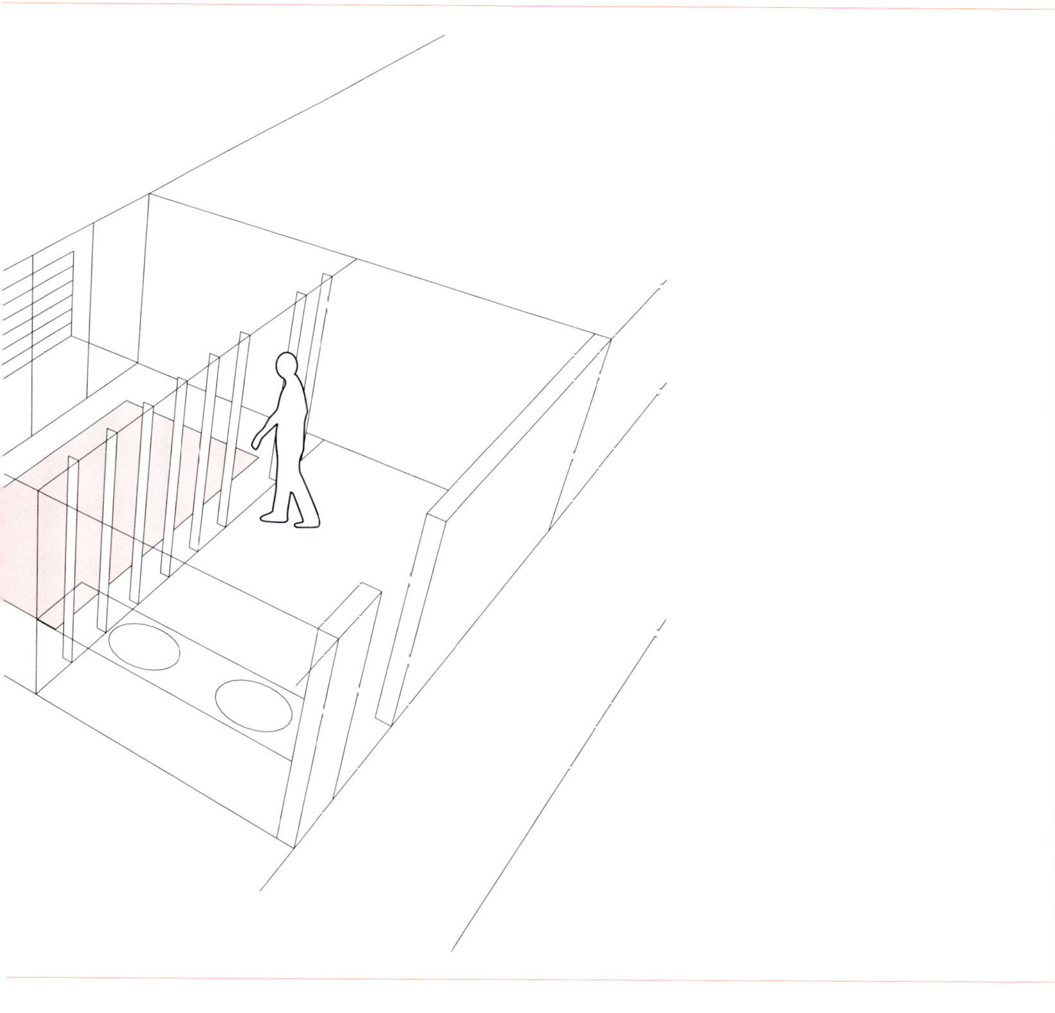

042
Co Kitchen

An empty apartment house is transformed into a common kitchen. Coupled with other facilities such as a laundry and a Co Bath, it responds to the danchi's collective function.

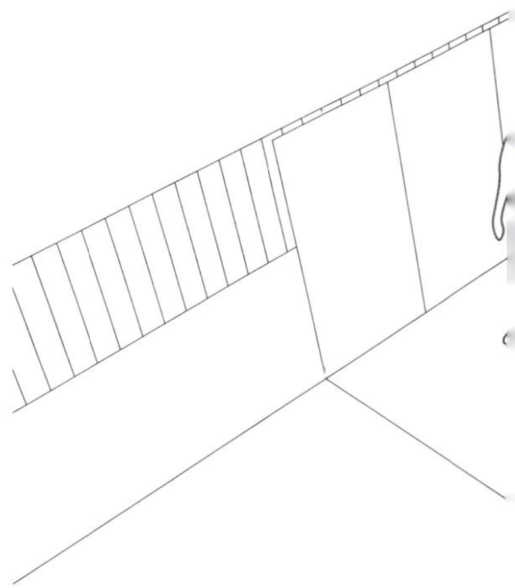

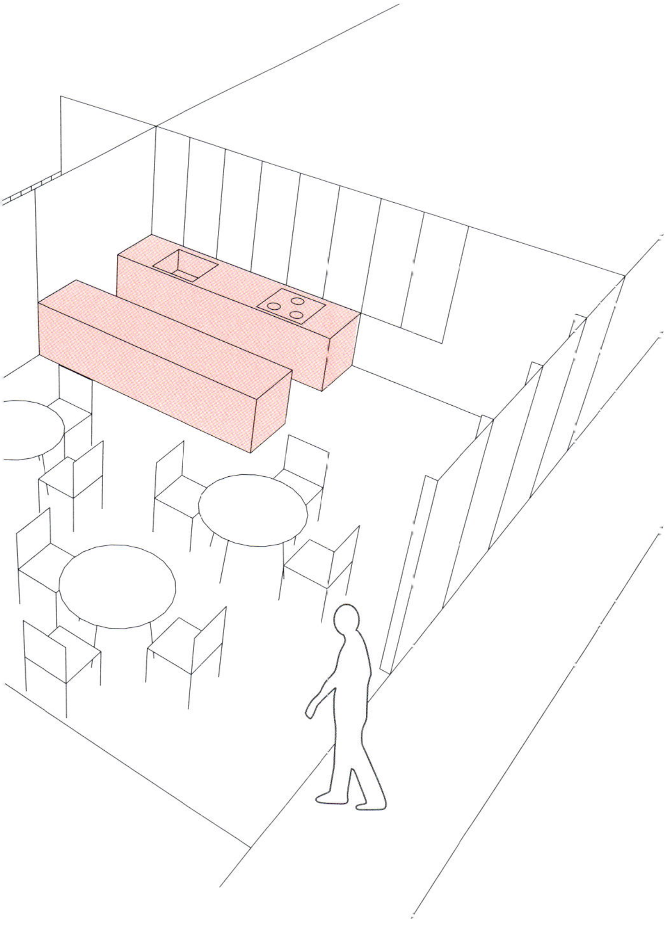

043
Rain Bath

Many devices in the danchi can find a new life within the estate itself. Here, old bathtubs no longer in use are collected and fixed to the roof to collect rainwater. The water is then used to water plants.

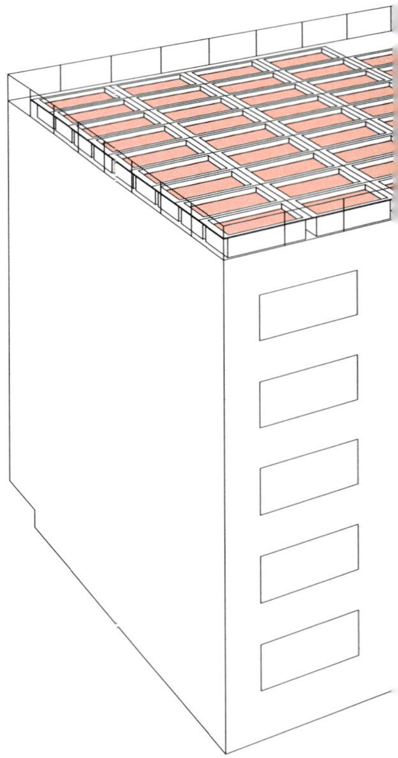

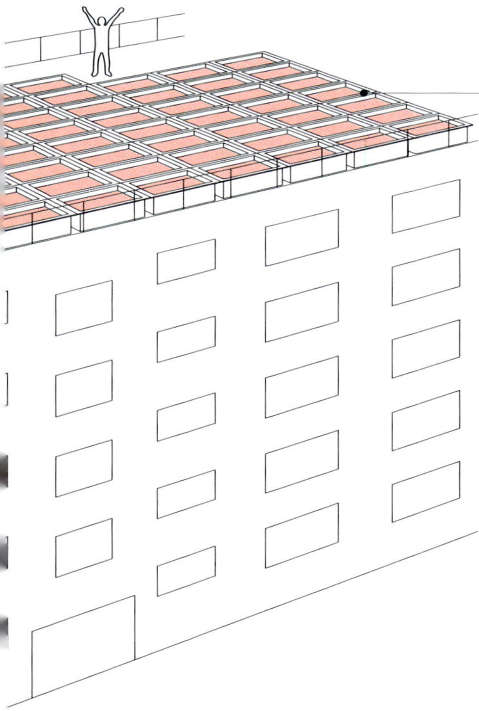

A former bathtub recycled
as a tank for rainwater

044
Door to Door

The old steel entrance doors are being recycled. Though they are heavy and sometimes hard to open, they are strongly built. Moreover danchi apartments are small and lack storage space. Therefore, new warehouses are implemented that use the steel doors as structural panels.

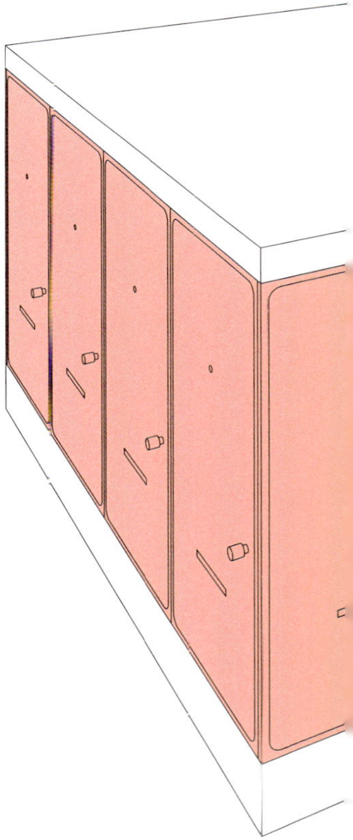

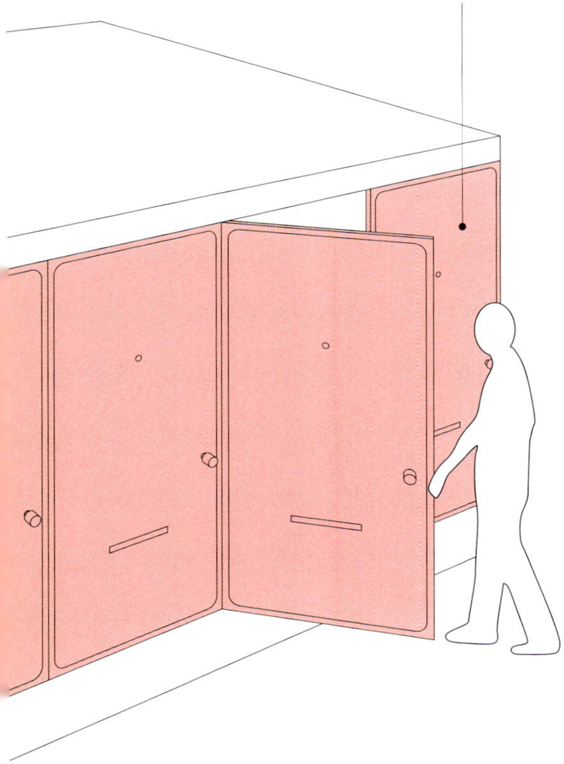
Former entrance doors recycled for storage facility

045 Flush the Flowers

Old Japanese toilets are being recycled like ready-made objects. This is an idea similar to the recycling of old tubs (see item 043). Here, the old Japanese-style toilets, which were replaced by newer models in each apartment, are used as flowerpots.

Toilets recycled as flowerpots for rooftop planting

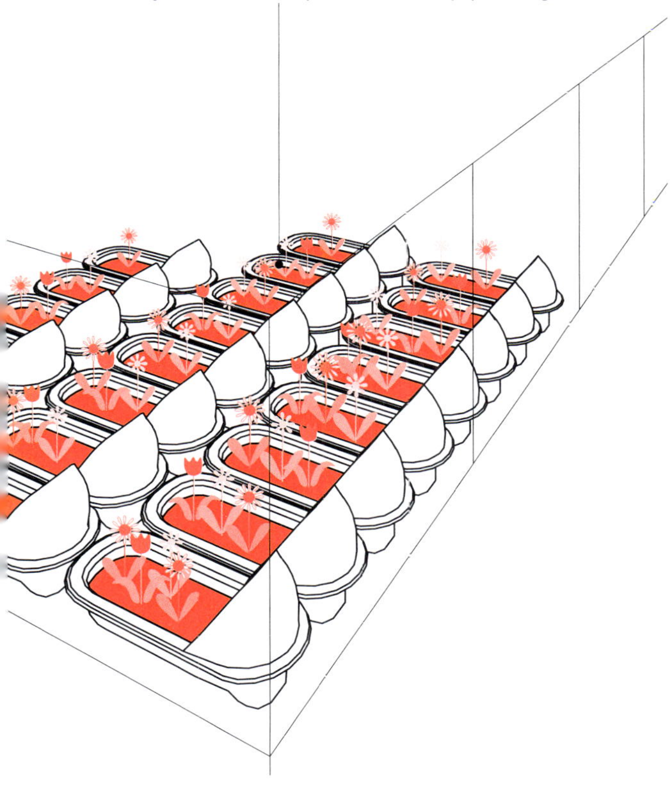

046
Danchi Block

Parts of the concrete outer walls and floor slabs, which are no longer needed when a housing unit is restructured, can be recycled after being taken down. Materials for flooring or gravel are easy to reuse for panels to make outer walls. Moreover, the unique history and atmosphere of the danchi remains visible within the recycled materials.

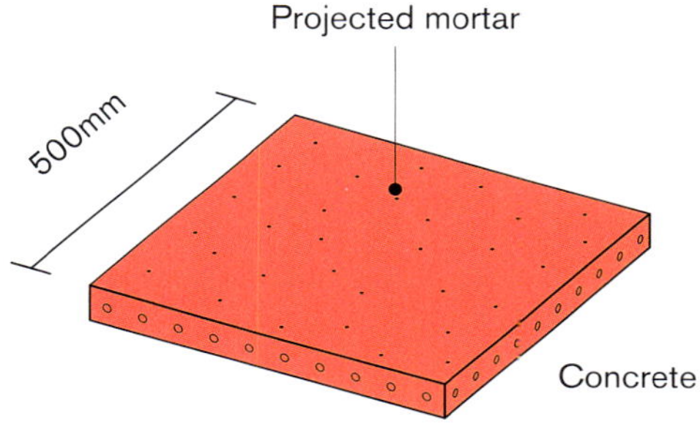

Section showing the reinforcing rods
→ surface of the rods washed with acid

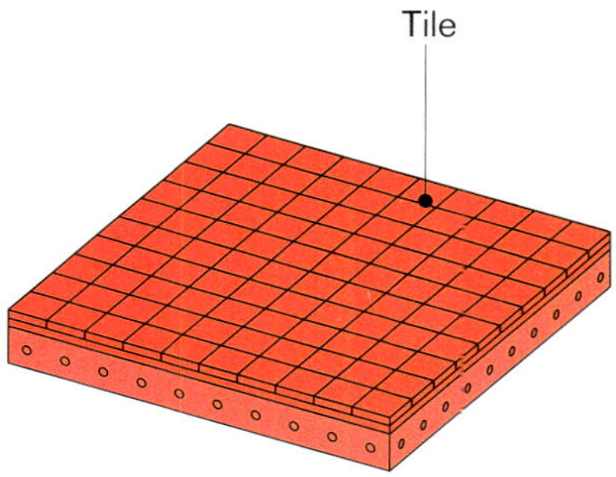

- Parts of outer walls or floor slabs that are recycled
- Materials for flooring or gravels
- Outer wall made of panels
- Fixing of tiles on the panels of the outer wall

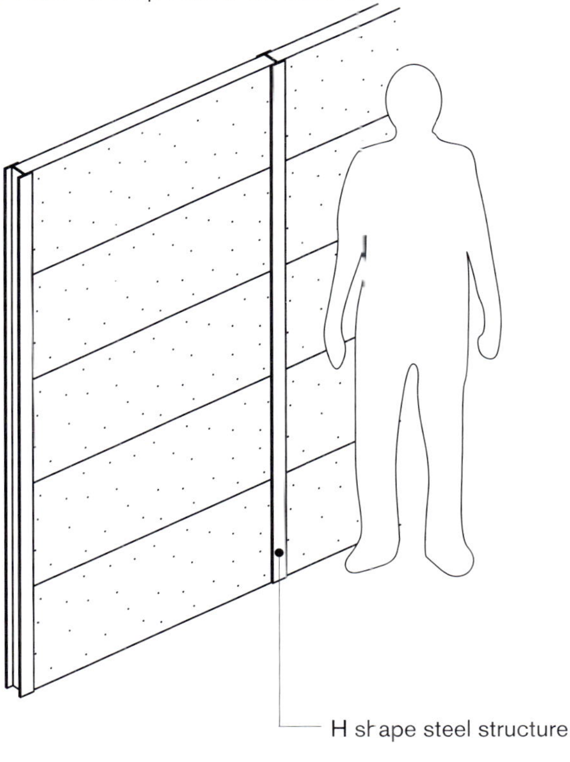

047
SOHO

The spread of personal computers allows a lot of work to be done at home. As a result, SOHO (Small Office House Office) housing units are increasing. However, it remains difficult to secure a space for meetings, and many organizational problems arise in these small spaces. SOHO units should perform more effectively. Here, a common meeting space fully equipped with home delivery boxes, copy, fax, and printing machines is set up.

Present condition

Type-A
Several apartment houses share a common space that is linked to a part of the balconies and the corridor

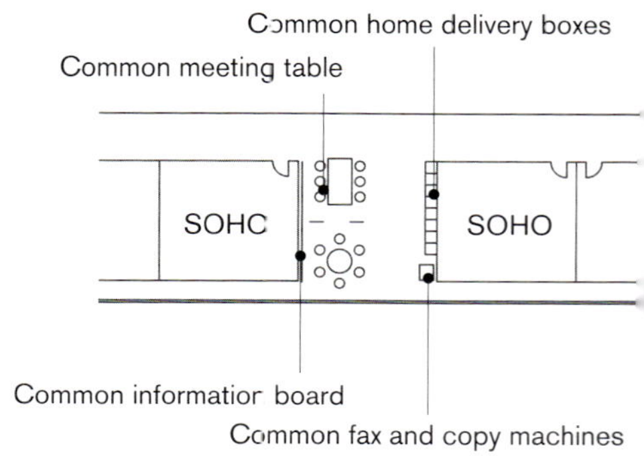

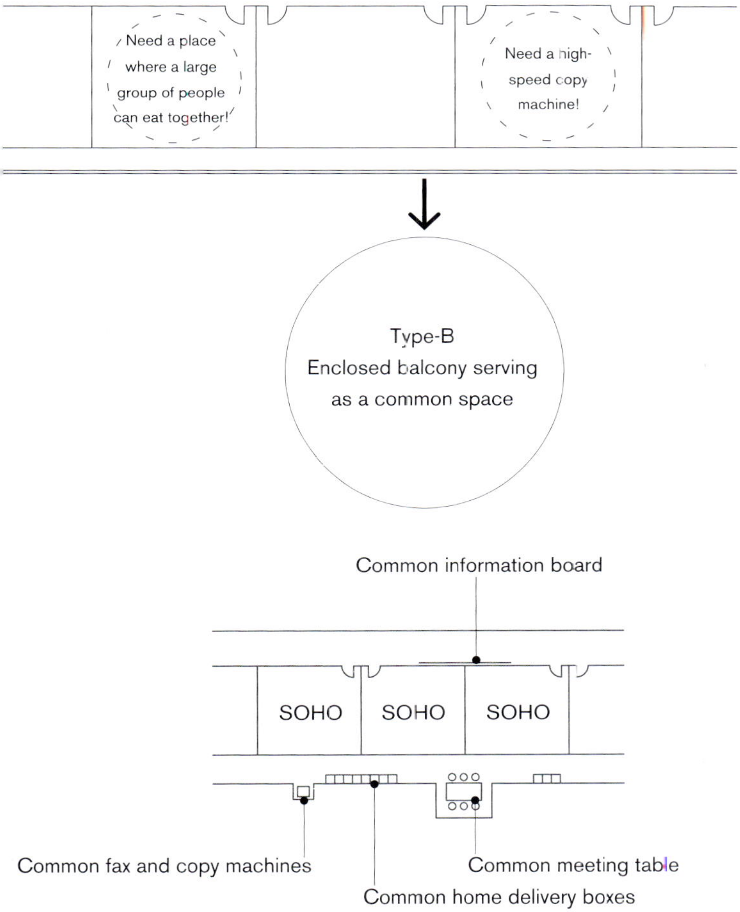

Need a place where a large group of people can eat together!
Need a high-speed copy machine!
Type-B
Enclosed balcony serving as a common space
Common information board
SOHO
SOHO
SOHO
Common fax and copy machines
Common meeting table
Common home delivery boxes

048 Rest the Guests

A single housing unit is dismantled and turned into a place that offers a new form of cohabitation. Rooms such as a salon and a club will be used as gathering places for young people. Corridors and balconies will become inner rooms when closed by sashes. Partitions will be minimized, creating a large space similar to a training camp. A kitchen and sinks will be installed in the former corridor, which forms a continuous space with the adjacent apartment.

A single housing unit serves as a training camp! The smallness of each apartment house disappears as it is divided into a series of private rooms.

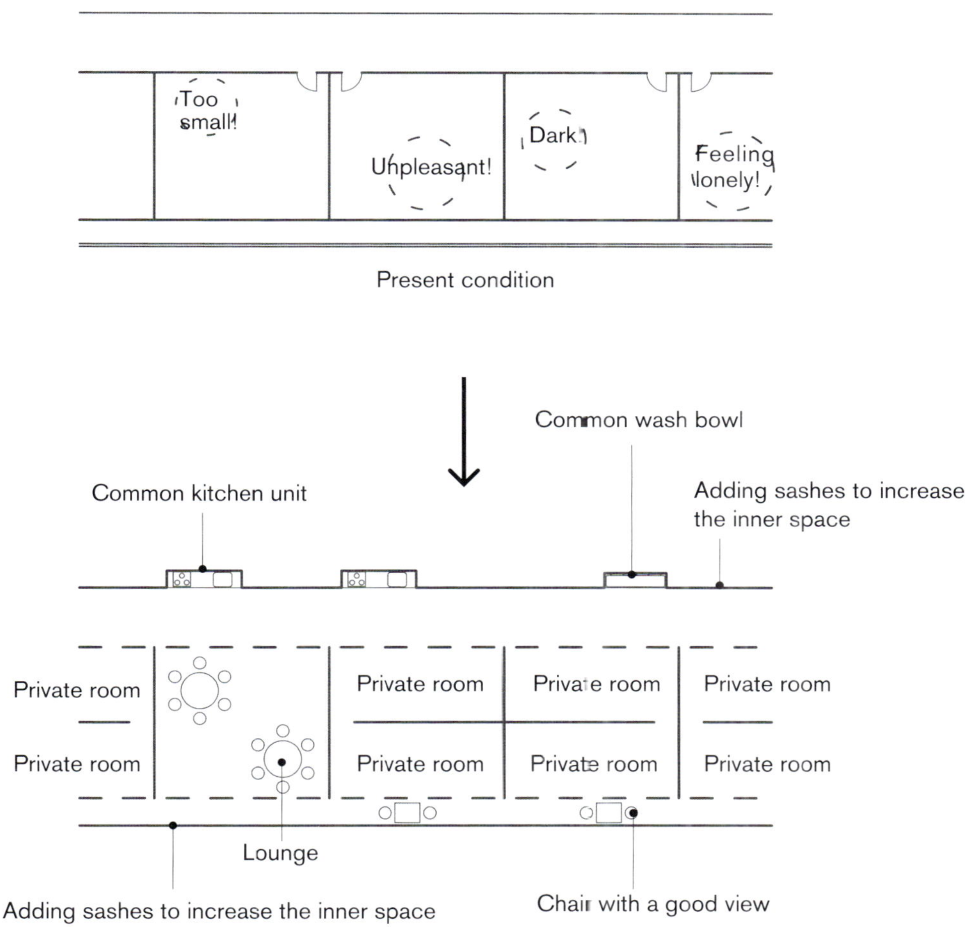

Too small!
Unpleasant!
Dark!
Feeling lonely!
Present condition
Common wash bowl
Common kitchen unit
Adding sashes to increase the inner space
Private room
Private room
Private room
Private room
Private room
Private room
Private room
Private room
Lounge
Adding sashes to increase the inner space
Chair with a good view

049 Atelier Danchi

It is hard for young artists in Japan to find places to work. As a result, obsolete danchi could provide suitable spaces entirely devoted to various kinds of ateliers—such as studios with complete soundproofing for musicians, or rooms with double height for sculptors. In the space between the housing units, outdoor concerts and exhibitions can be held for all of the local residents.

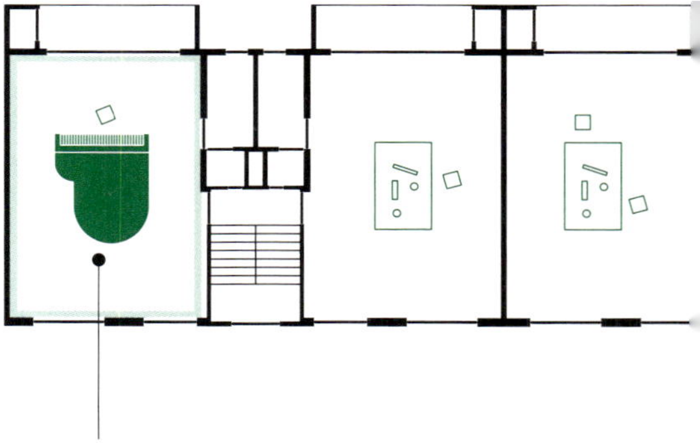

Rooms after being soundproofed are transformed into studios for musicians

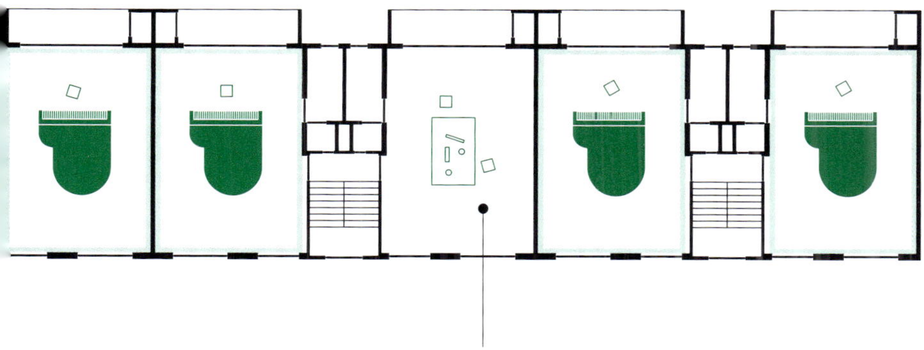

After removing all inner partitions, a single apartment is transformed into an atelier for painters

050 High-Rise Garden

There is little room for open spaces within the high-rise danchi in urban areas. Thus, the staircases that are used routinely by people could also be used as a park. Slabs of the staircases and elevator shafts provide adequate spaces for implementing vertical gardens.

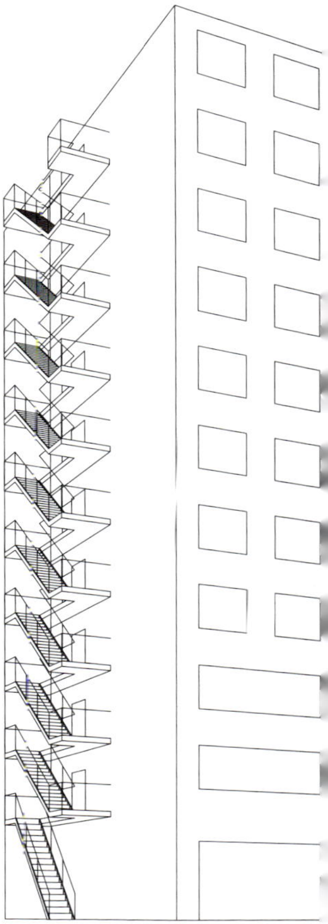

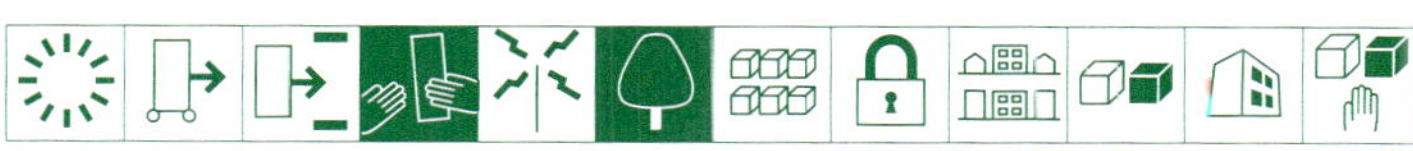

051 Private Garden

In a danchi, it is difficult for residents to own a private garden. Nevertheless, there are various ways of providing spaces for individual gardens, such as removing an apartment and replacing it, using the flat roof, or the large open spaces of the ground floor. Creating such places requires preparation like installing water supply and drainage systems, bringing lightweight soil, and reinforcing the structures of the existing housing units. The variety of gardens helps create a luxuriant outside space and naturally expresses the different tastes, and even the regionalism, of its inhabitants.

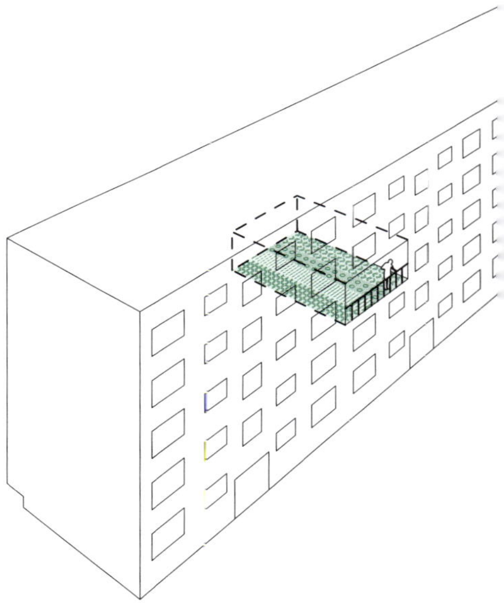

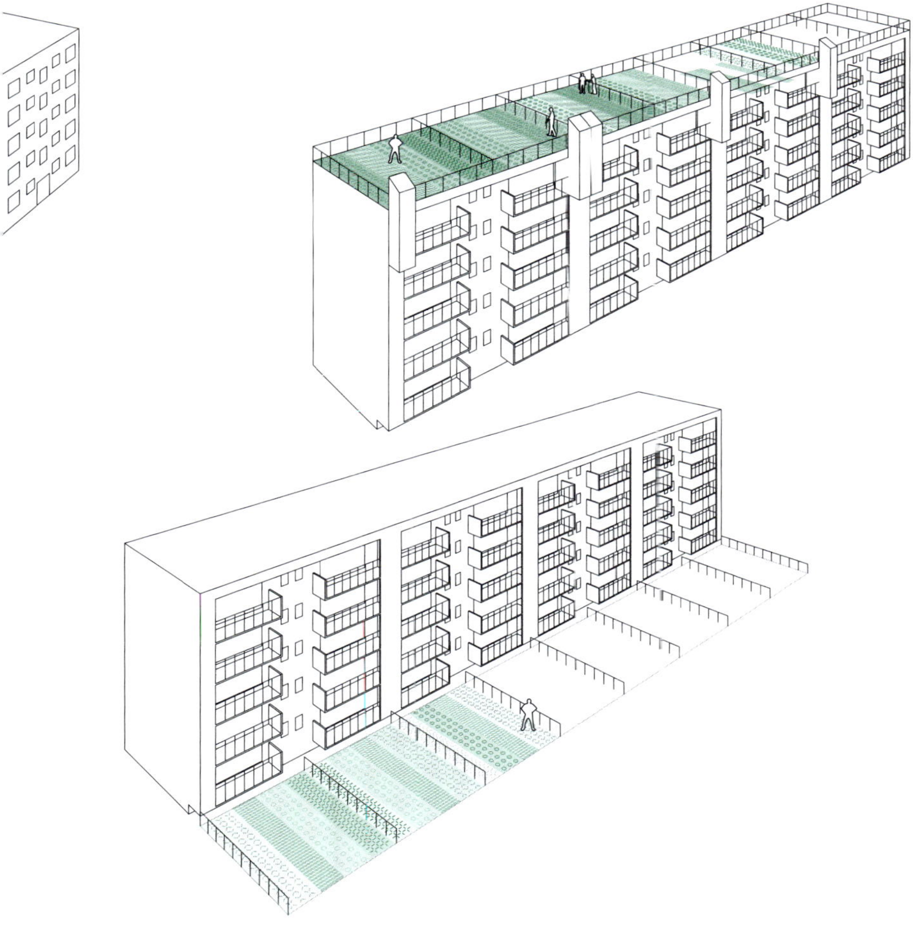

052 Mail-Go-Round

Danchi post boxes are confusing and tasteless. For short elderly residents and children, mail is hard to retrieve. Transforming these boxes into a mail-go-round apparatus is fun and brings the boxes to a reasonable height. Mail is received by turning the steering wheel like a lottery machine.

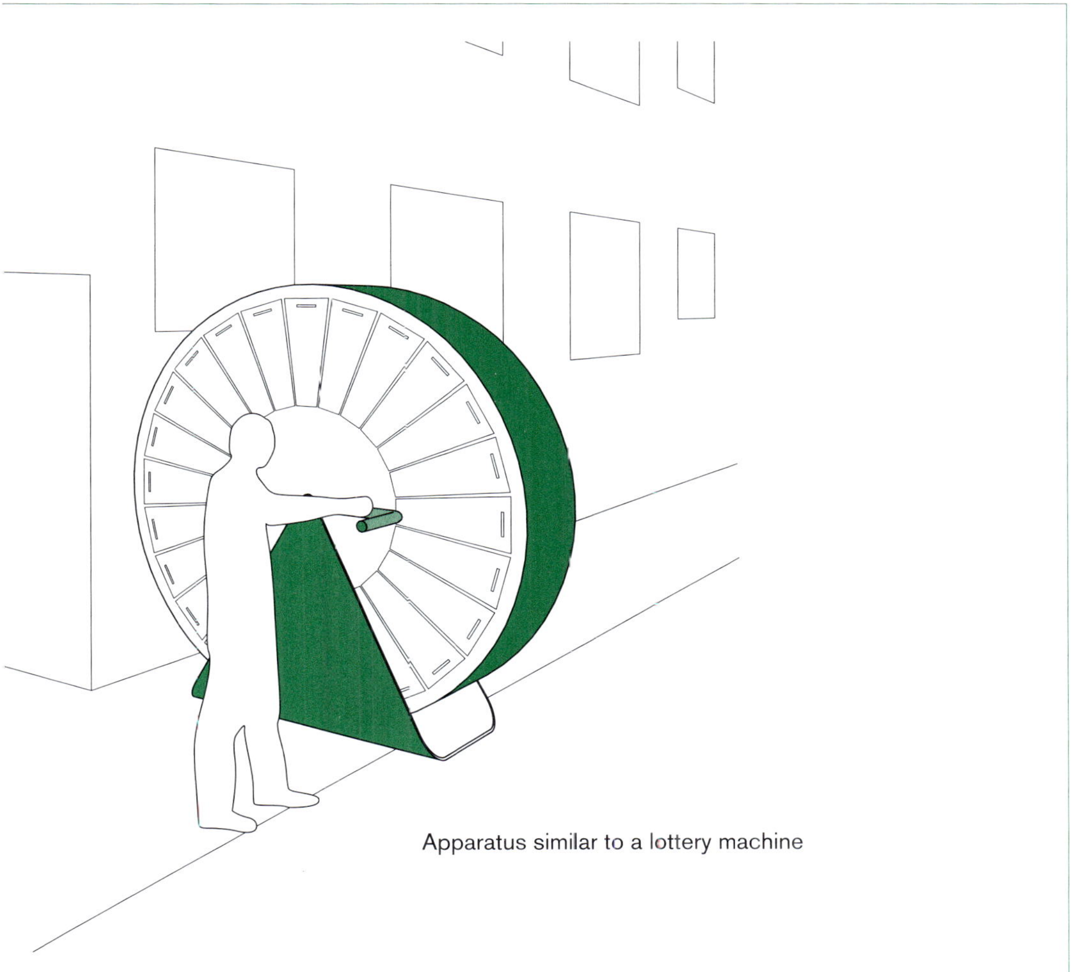

Apparatus similar to a lottery machine

053 Box in Box

One of the main reasons for the poor impression left by the entrance halls of the danchi is the mailboxes. The current situation seems to be the mediocre solutions given to such a function. These new mailboxes solve the problem by allowing the residents to freely select the material and color. This will help transmit personal feelings within the common space. It is also possible to take one's box as a memento when moving out.

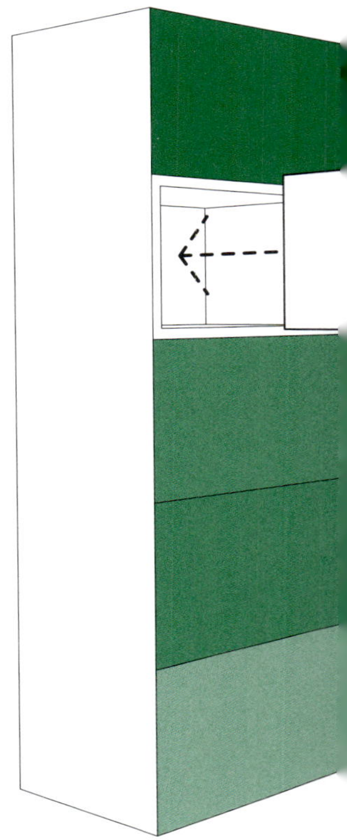

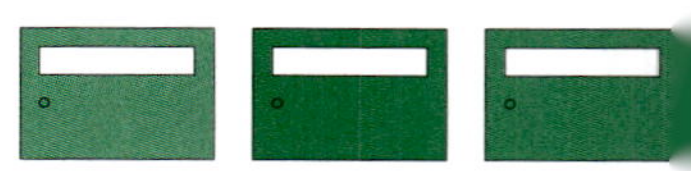

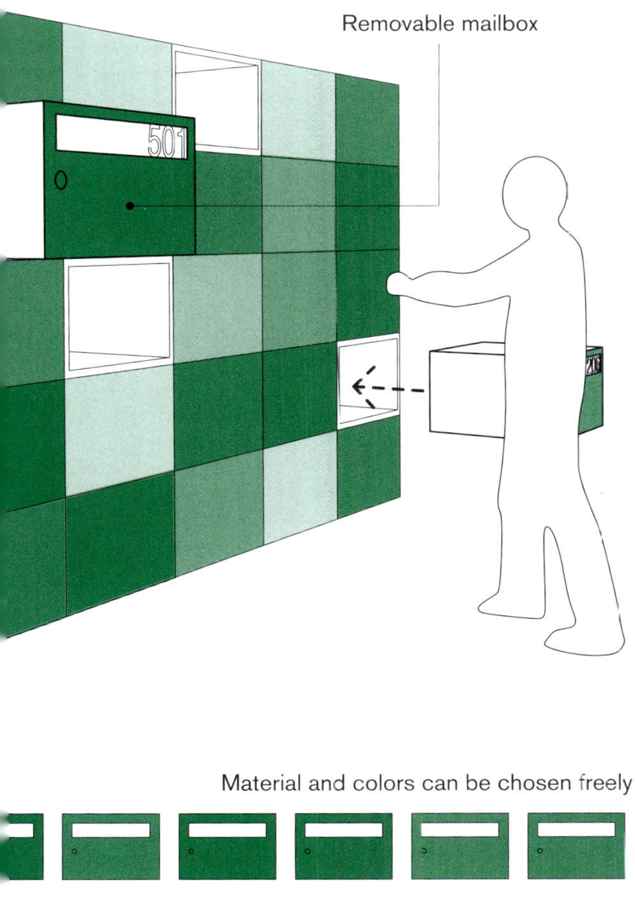
Removable mailbox
501
Material and colors can be chosen freely

054
Recycled Billboard

In the danchi, the garbage area is a necessity for all of the inhabitants. Consequently, this area can be used successfully for implementing a graphical information board. It will become an advertising space and a place for information exchange information between the inhabitants. The materials used for the board will be all recycled.

The surface of the wall is used as an information board
資源ゴミは大切に
ゴミの日は守りましょう

055 Sanit Unit

There is a large demand from the inhabitants for a variety of rooms equipped with water supply. In this scheme, each apartment is provided with a sanitary unit whose contents can be selected as desired. For maximum freedom, these units are superimposed within a substructure next to the housing unit.

● Toilet unit
This unit provides a restroom. Suppression of this function in the main body of the existing housing unit allows greater freedom for reorganizing rooms.
● Bath unit
This unit has a dressing room and a bathroom, and offers renewed comfort.
● Laundry unit
This unit is equipped with a washing machine and a drying room, which can also be used for other purposes.
● Spare unit
This type is adapted to fit the previous ones with freedom of use.

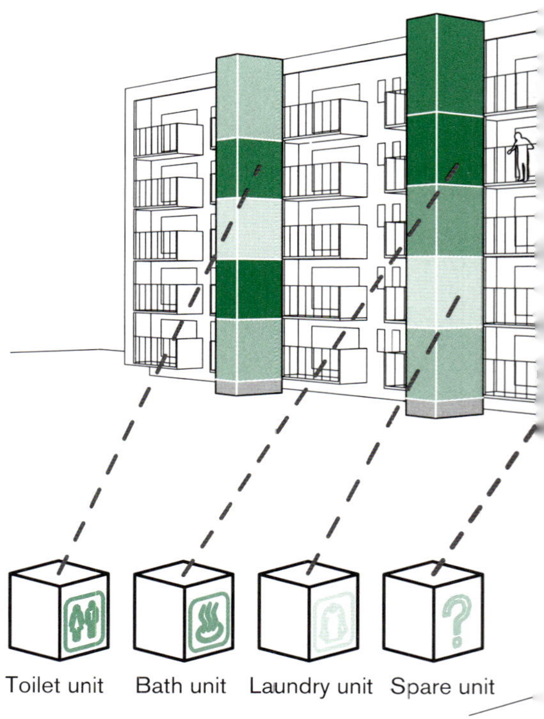

056 Sign House

The present entrance halls of the danchi are confusing and messy with their profusion of information. A separate building will house functions such as the mailboxes, information board, and the numbers and names of the apartment units. The new entrance addition not only gathers ads and signs but also proposes a new face for the revitalized danchi.

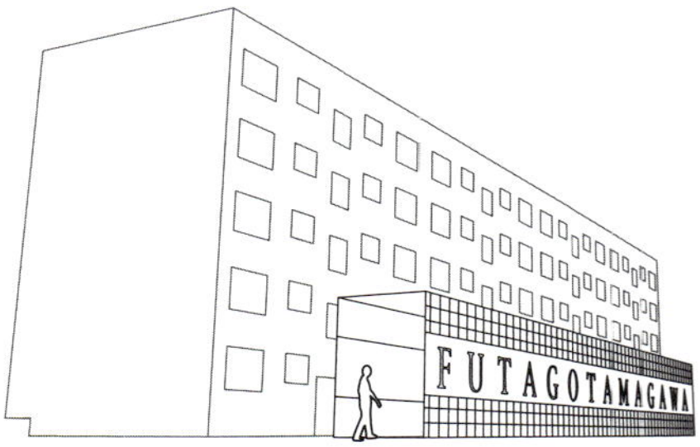

Mailboxes and an information board are installed

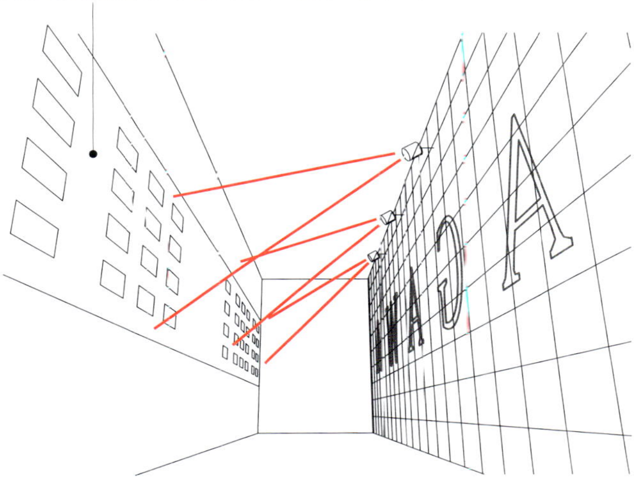

Lights up at night

057
Cover Tower

Outdoor units and the air-conditioner plumbing system are spoiling the façades of the danchi. Here is a proposal that hides these unappealing fixtures. An outer tower with a cover made of expanded metal, which is fixed to the outer wall, hides the outdoor units and the refrigerant pipes.

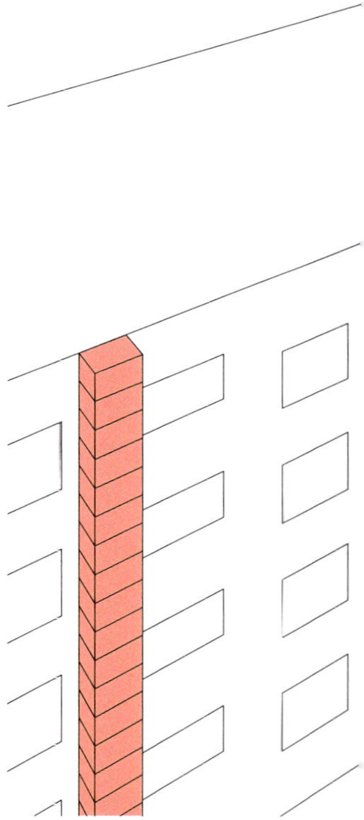

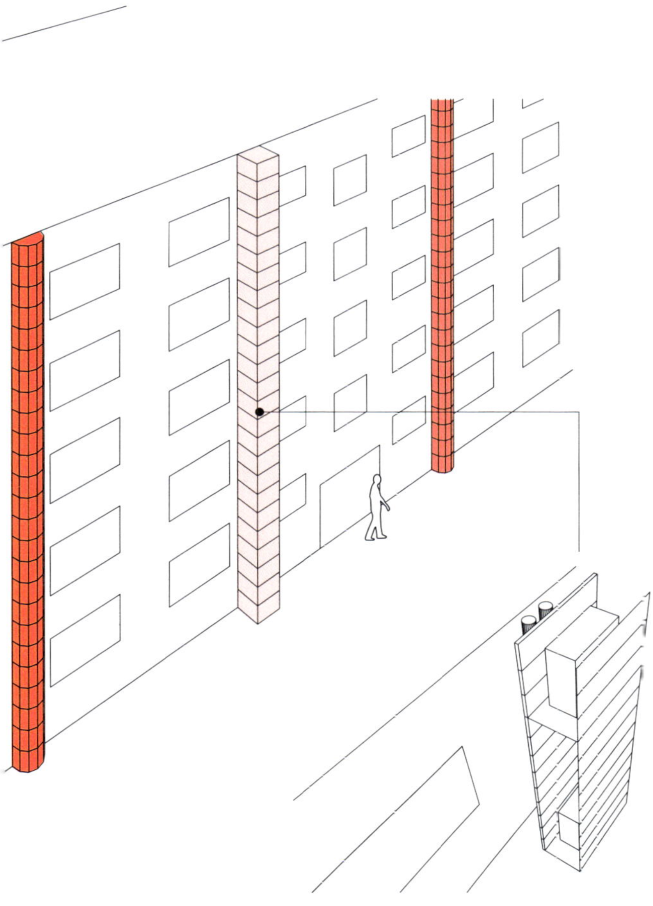

Outdoor units and pipes of the air-conditioners all covered

058 Under Cover

There are a lot of things stored on danchi balconies, such as outdoor units of air-conditioners and washing machines. Here, a cover hides them in one simple design. Even if one looks from inside, the apparatuses are hidden under the handrail of the balcony. Moreover, the handrails serve as planter boxes.

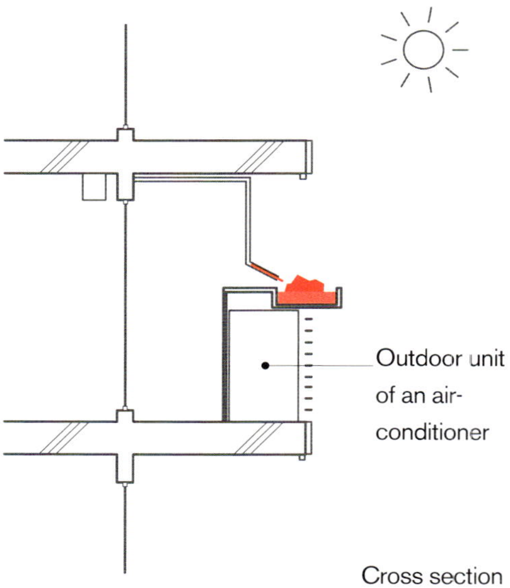

Cross section

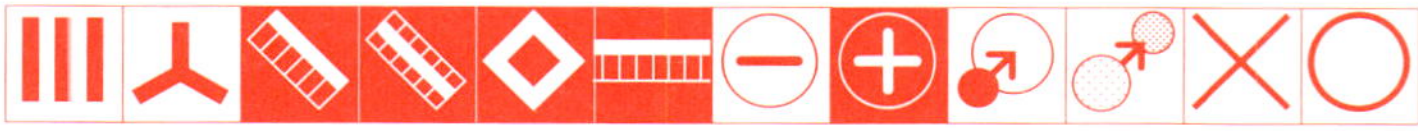

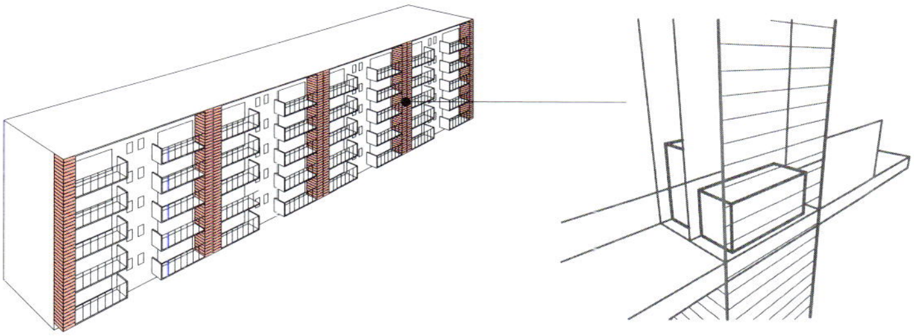

Covers for outdoor units, washing machines, etc.

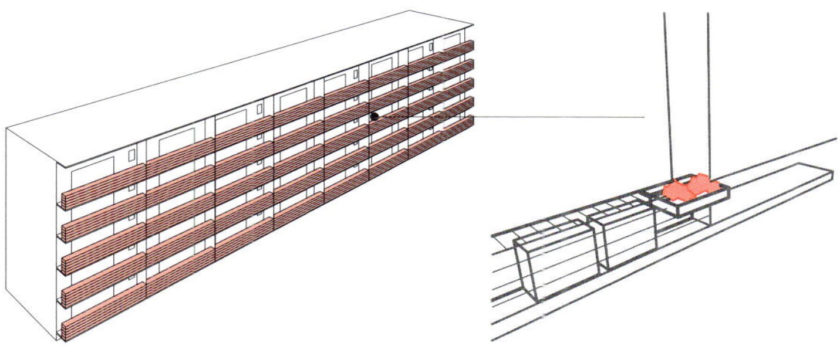

059 Zoo Balcony

It is forbidden to have pets in most danchi. Nevertheless, pets that do not make a lot of noise are sometimes secretly kept in special devices that cater to a variety of pets. After being waterproofed, the balcony will be enclosed like a bird cage. An adequate ventilation system will also be installed in this apartment. Eventually, the entire balcony will look like a kind of zco.

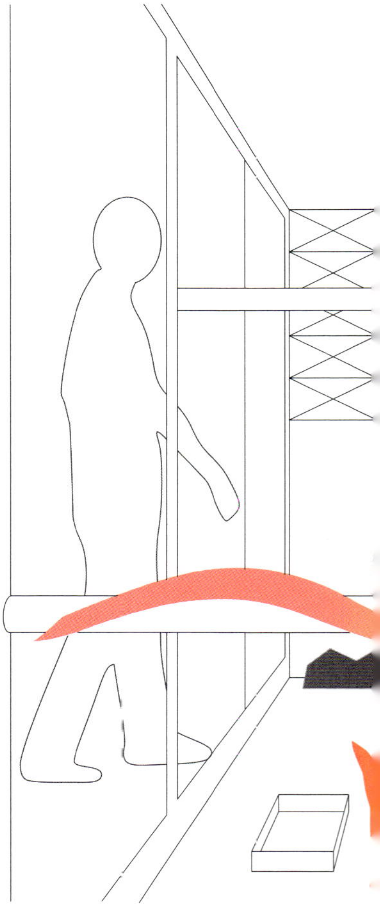

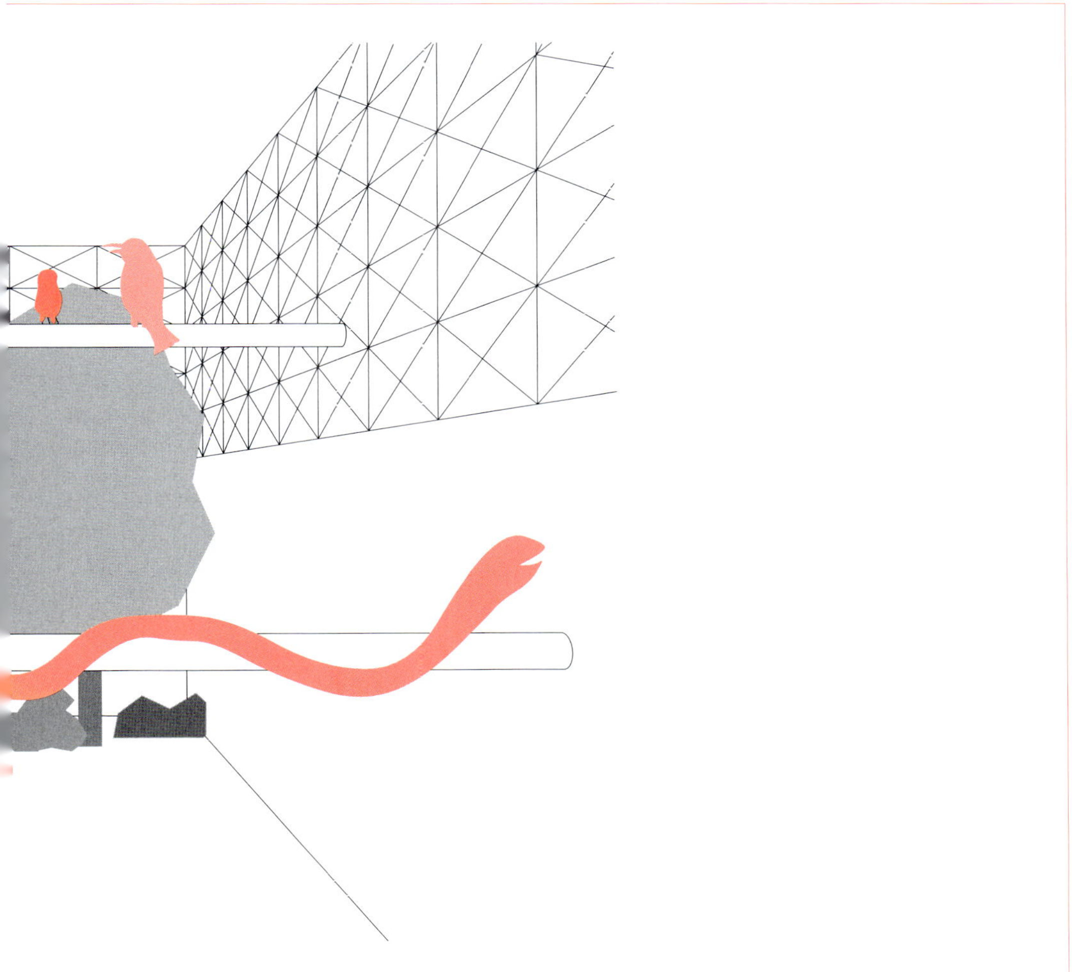

060
Big Bal

The use of the balconies in the danchi is usually restricted to the airing of laundry. Therefore, creating an external structure that enlarges balconies can extend the possibilities of use. Then each inhabitant is free to enjoy his balcony like a private garden.

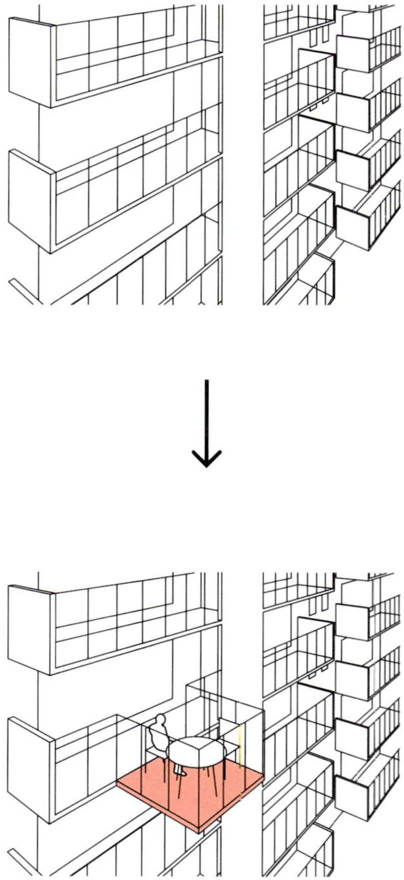

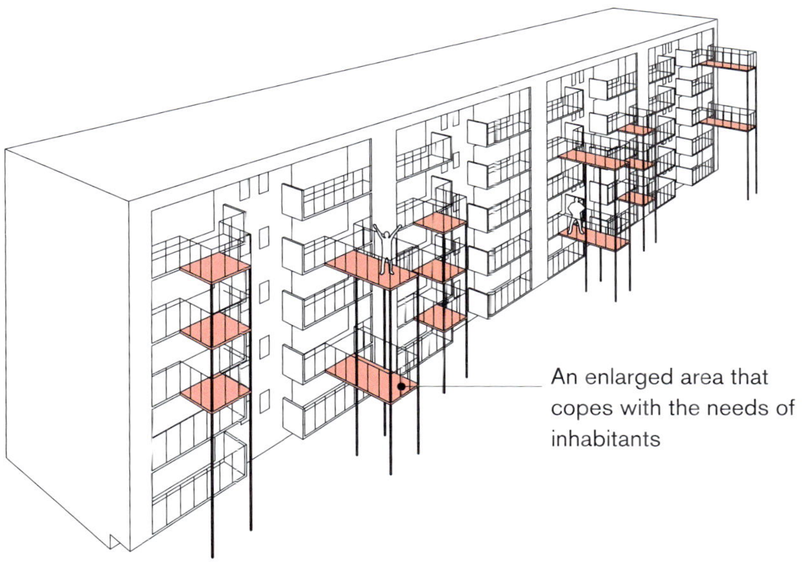
An enlarged area that copes with the needs of inhabitants

061 My Beautiful Balcony

Danchi apartments are very narrow. A system that even slightly increases floor space will be welcome. Changing a balcony that functions only as an area for drying clothes into part of the interior of a flat responds to a demand made by the residents. The design of the panels enclosing the balconies will allow various functions and revive the expression of the danchi.

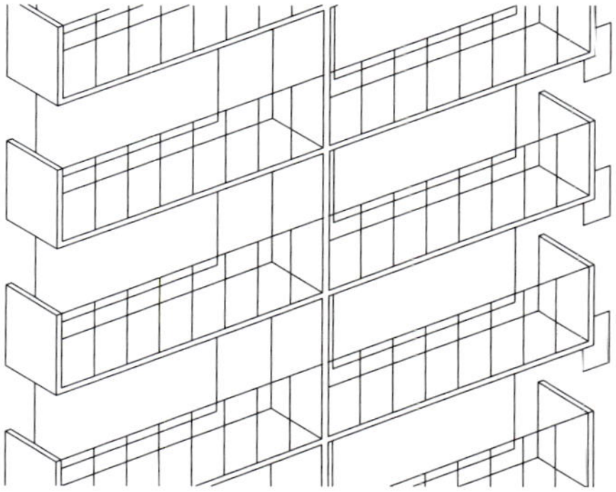

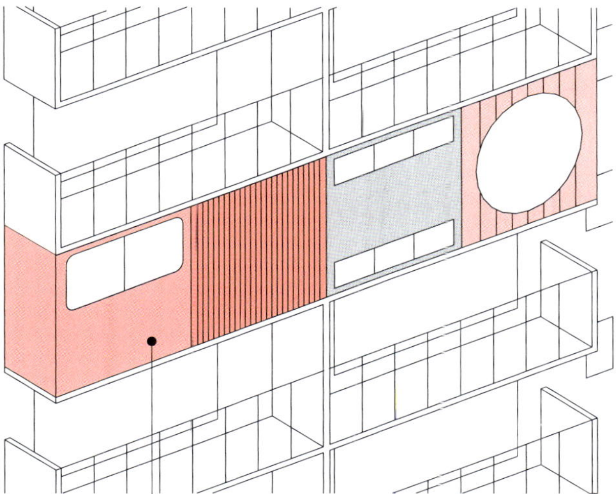

Façade as the result of a selection responding to various tastes and uses

062 Baroom

Danchi apartments are very narrow. Sometimes, however, inhabitants need a place to host temporary guests. A folding system of inflated panels with good insulation can enclose the balcony—which usually functions as a place to dry clothes—to create an additional room. When not in use, the panels can be compacted and stored.

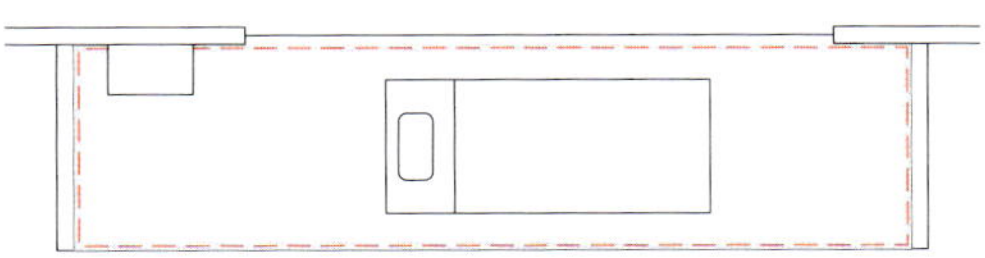

Extra room on the balcony enclosed by panels with good insulation
Inflating panels

063 Kit Cut

This aim of this system is the easy transformation of a typical single-story danchi unit into a duplex apartment.
A stair kit with a cover made of lightweight FRP is fixed to the balcony of a flat. This connects two flats transforming them into one single duplex apartment.
The kit can also provide a large window.

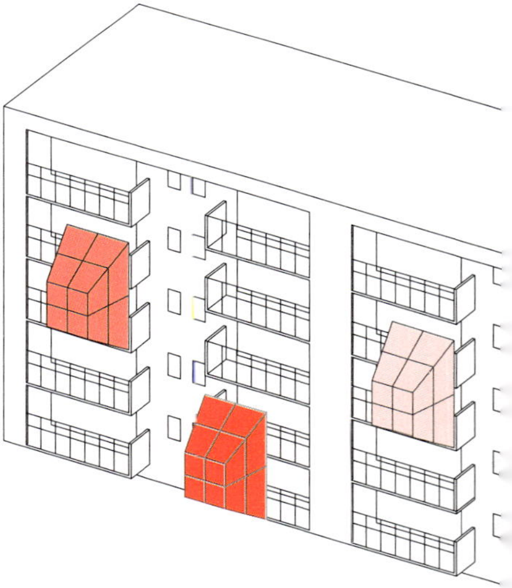

An easy kit for a duplex apt

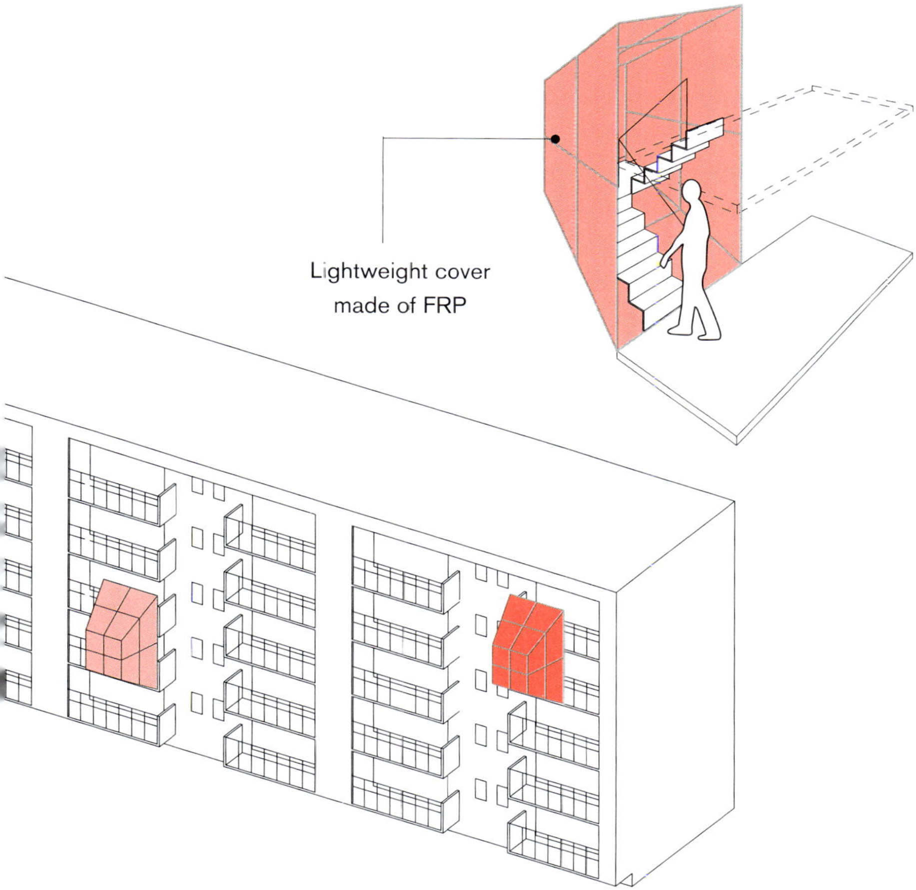
Lightweight cover
made of FRP

064 Mind the Curtains

Installing exterior curtains in front of balconies and windows offers several advantages. Balconies can become extra rooms, and curtains also help to reduce the amount of heat due to direct sunlight. They also create more privacy and change the exterior expression of a housing unit with their movement and various fabrics.

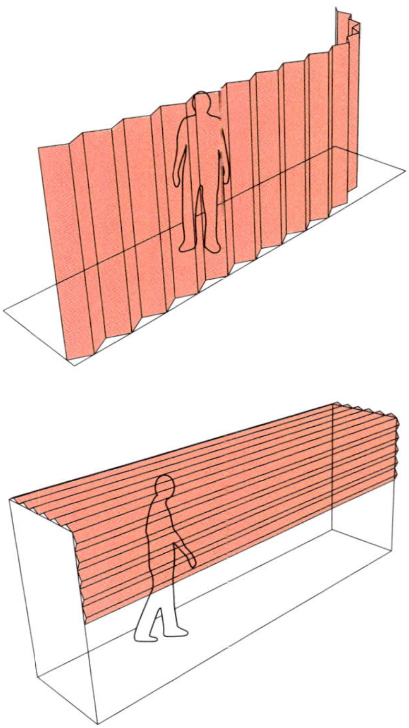

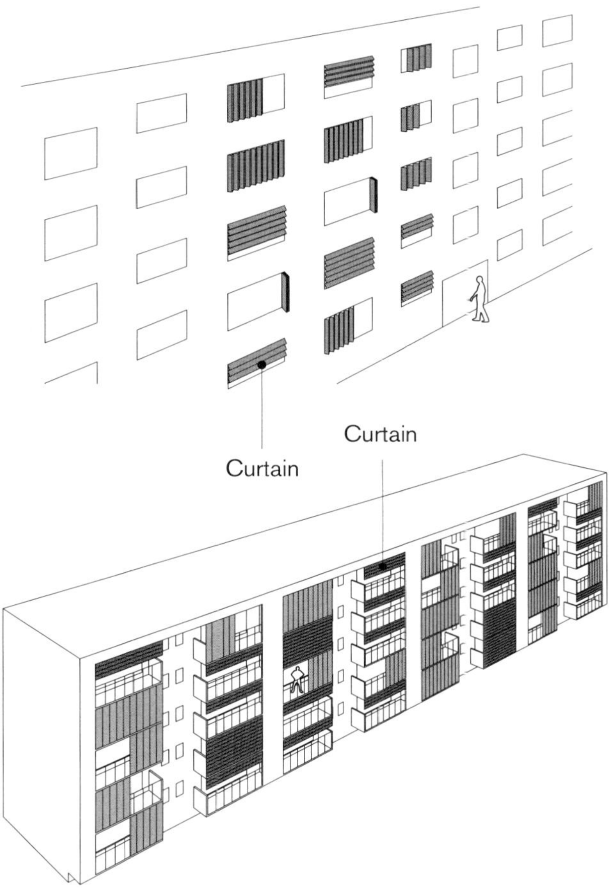
Curtain
Curtain

065
Outer Dryer

A cage made of steel rods is fixed in front of an opening allowing its enlargement. Its function is similar to a bay-window. A roof or poles for clothes can also be added if necessary.

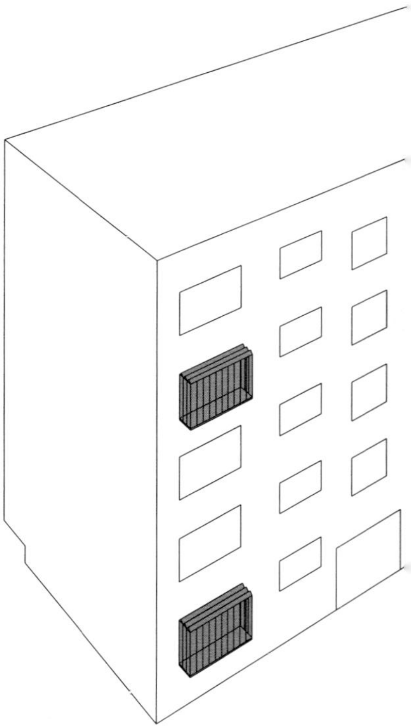

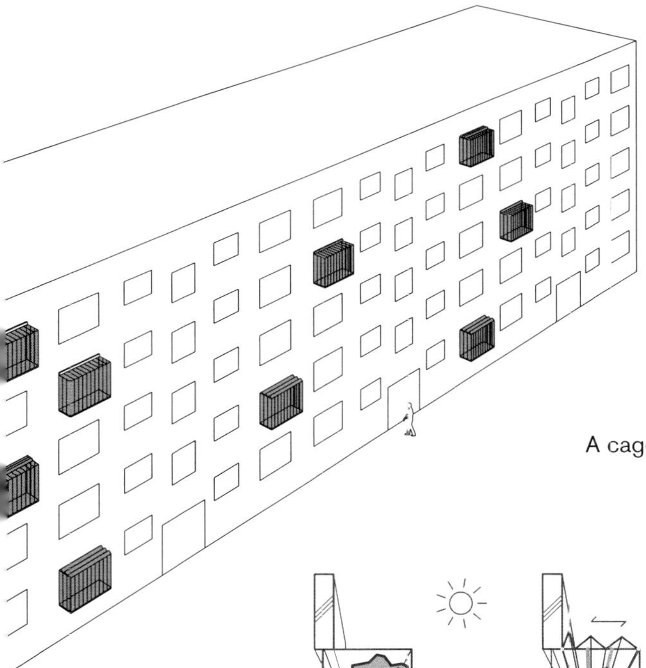

A cage with a roof or poles for clothes

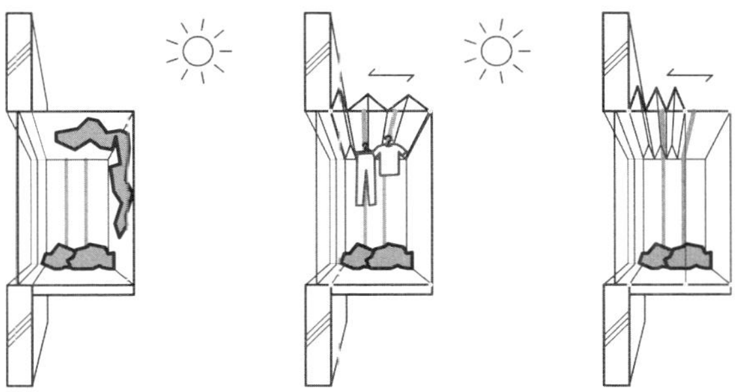

066
Full Open Window

Folding doors that open completely allow the use of the entire balcony. Unlike sliding doors, balconies become semi-outdoor extensions of the apartments with these devices. In combination with Domani (item 071), more attractive balcony spaces are now a reality.

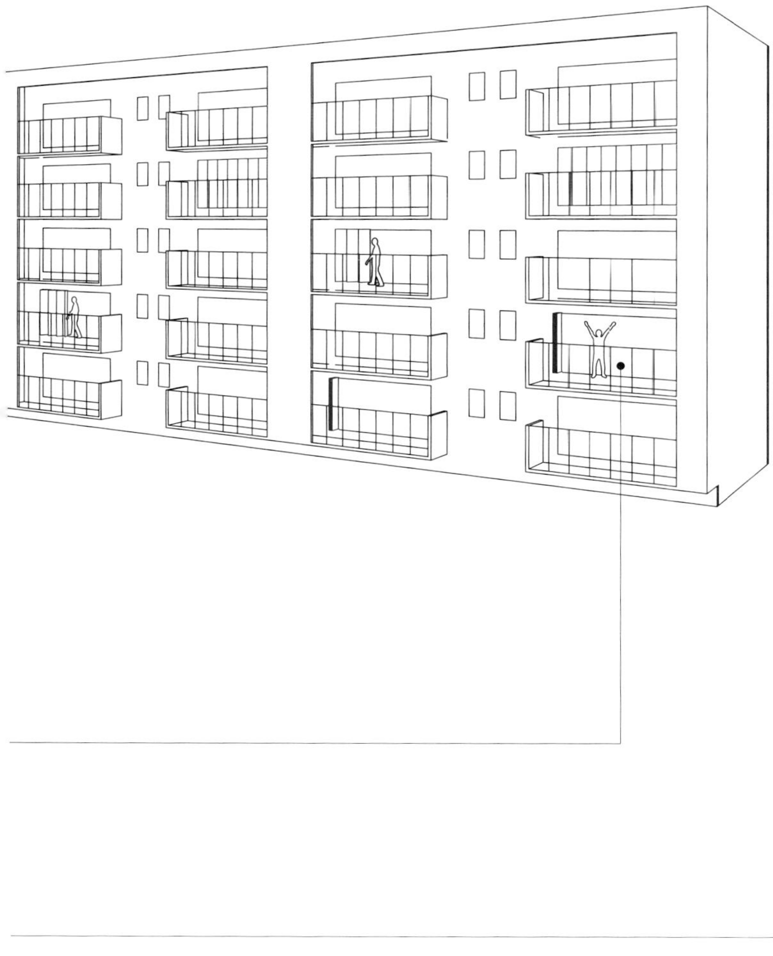

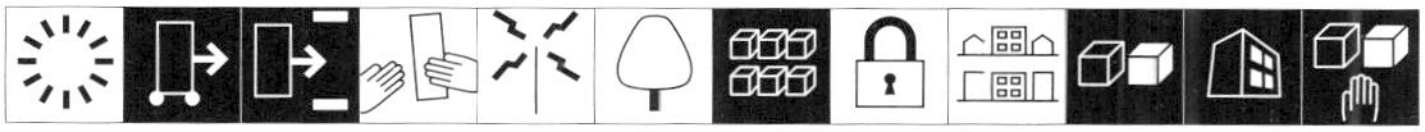

067 Rolling Dryer

Daily housework represents a big burden for housewives. Therefore, this new apparatus is a convenient tool allowing laundry to be aired on the balcony without leaving the room just by turning a pole. Made of metal it can support weight as heavy as a futon (traditional Japanese bed blankets).

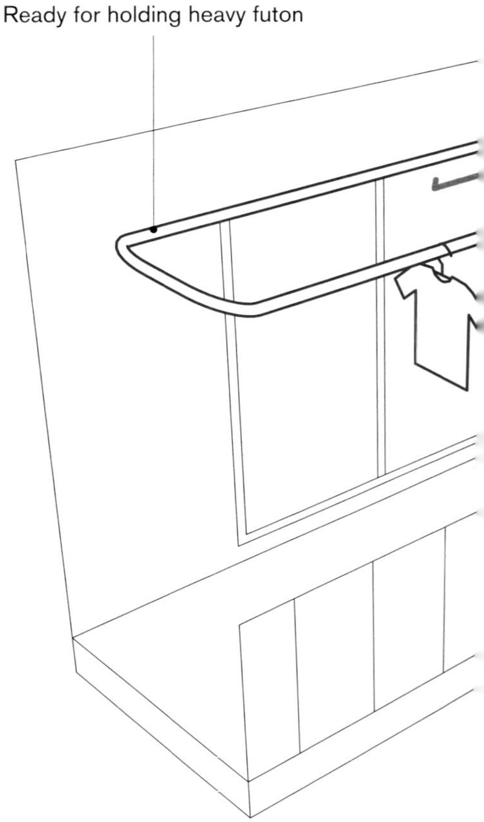

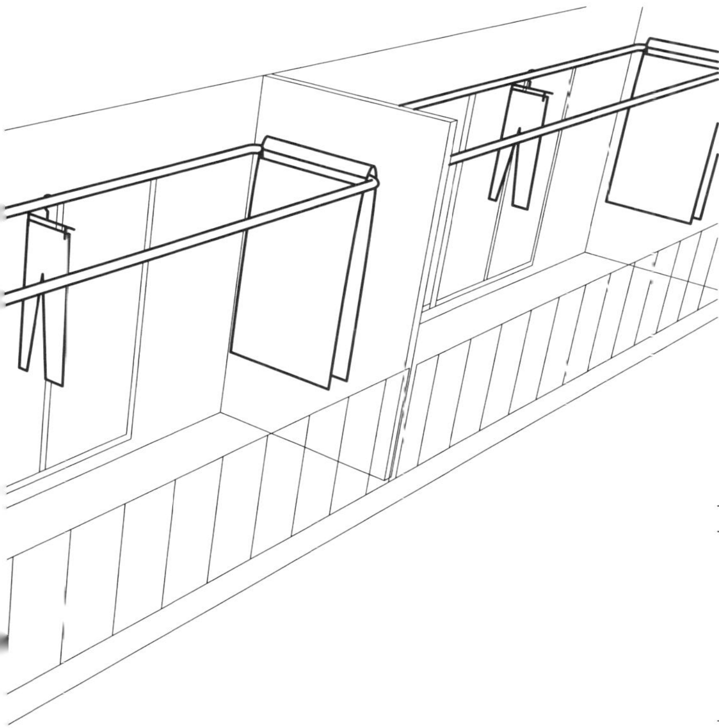

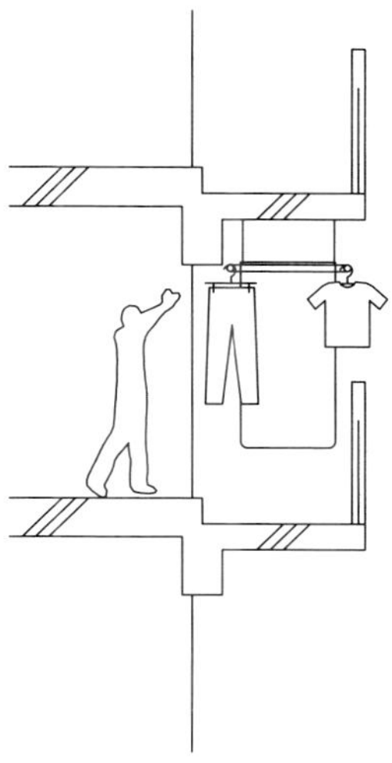

068
Passive I

A passive solar system is implemented by using the danchi balconies as a double wall. This system provides energy savings for the housing units as well as increased comfort. Oriel windows promote ventilation through a draft effect in the summer and retain warm air in winter with a heat storage floor.

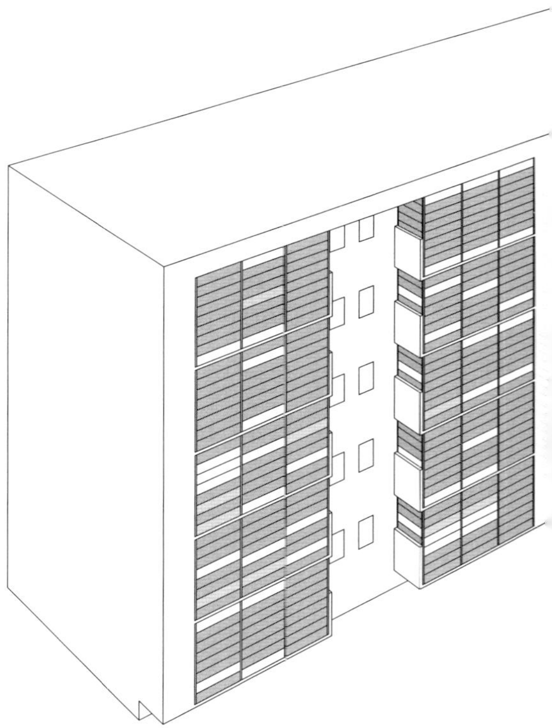

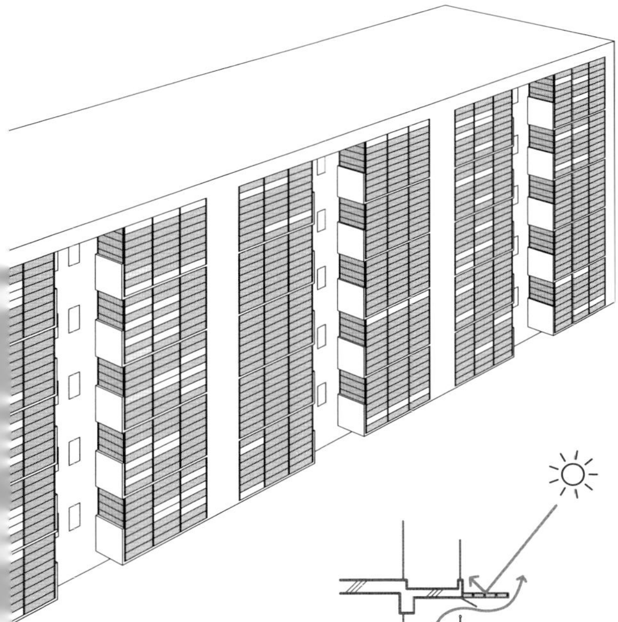

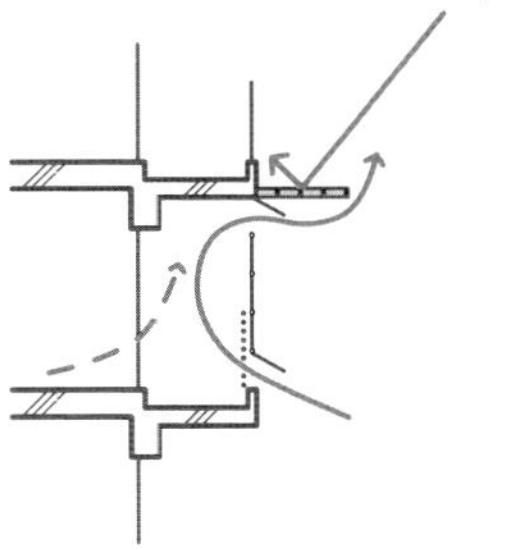

Ventilation through draft effect

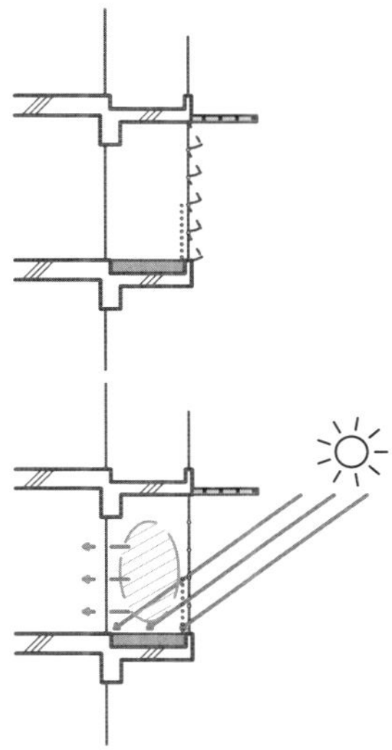

Heat storage floor at night
in the summer
Heat storage floor in the winter

069
Shop & Door

Apartments in the danchi can be transformed into small retail stores by simply replacing the walls of their entrances with a signboard and their doors with counters. Three-dimensional commercial areas in the estate change the atmosphere of the housing units, which become more like parts of a city.

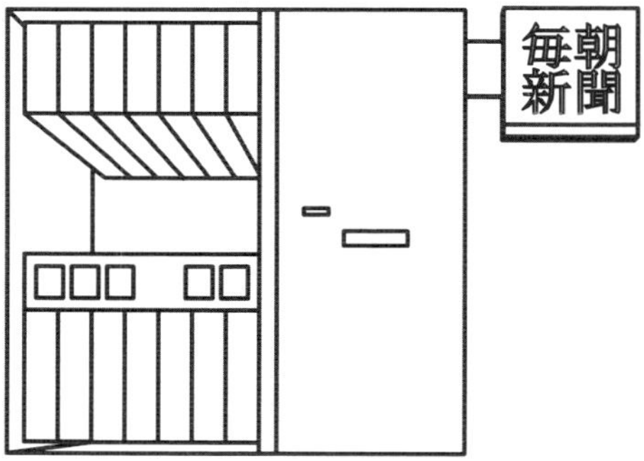

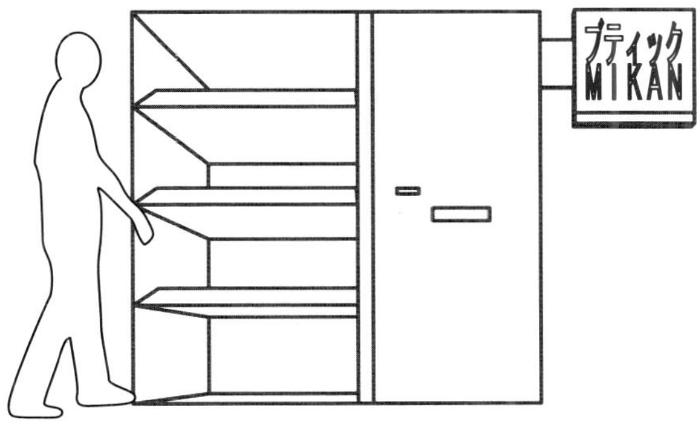
ブティック
MIKAN

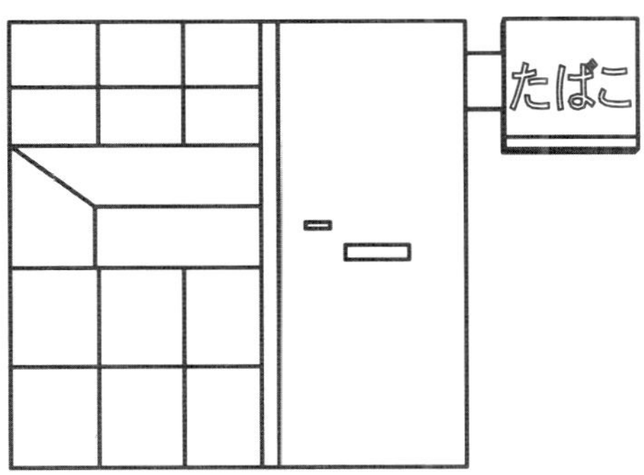
たばこ

070
Living Module System

This series of furniture and kitchen units match the basic module system of the danchi. By sharing a constant dimension in their depth and a similar finishing on their sides and backs, this furniture can also be used for partitioning. The furniture eventually replaces all partitioning for a one-room apartment and adapts to various kinds of lifestyles. In addition, there is a shower unit that can be folded when not in use, making it very convenient as it minimizes wet rooms within these small apartments.

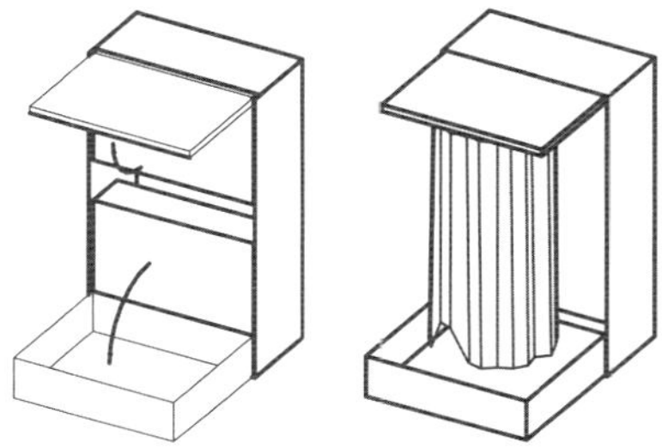

Shower unit

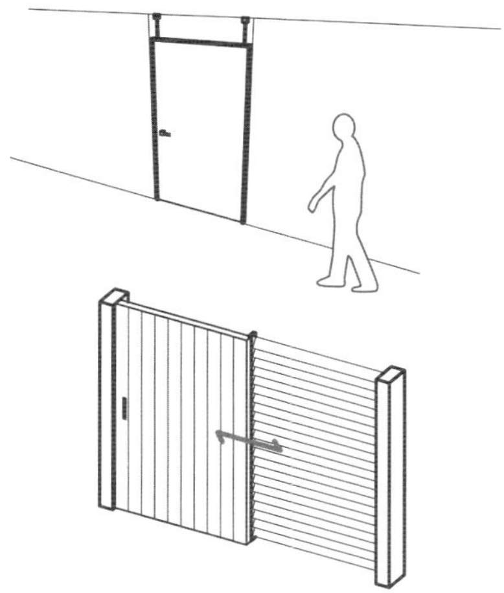

Entrance sliding door unit

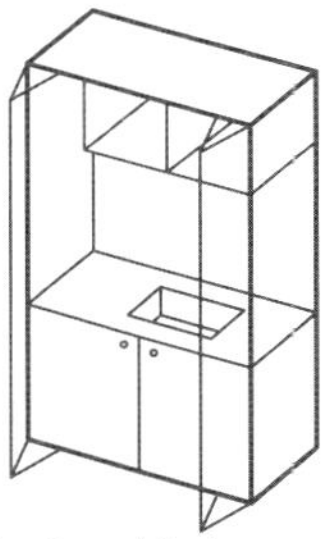

System kitchen unit

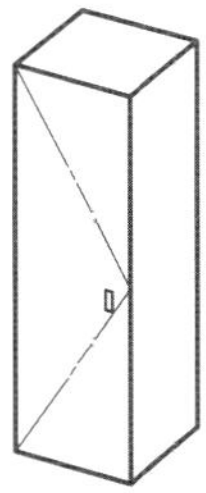

Storage unit

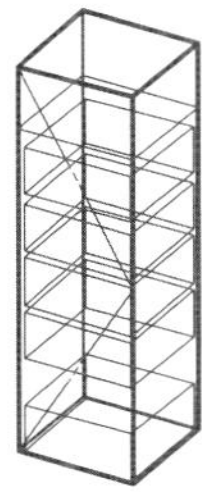

Drawer unit

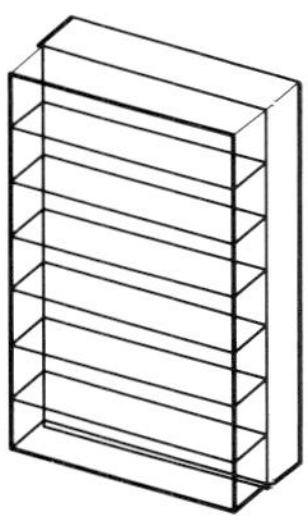

Bookshelf unit

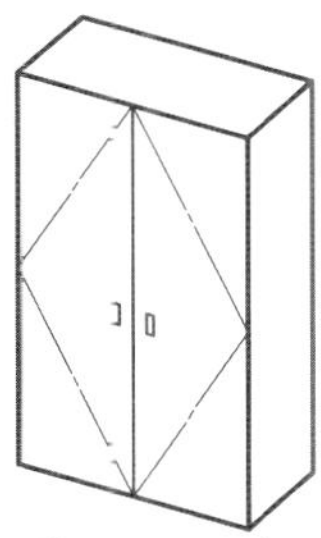

Storage unit

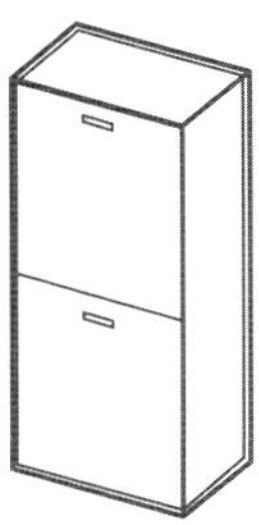

Writing table unit

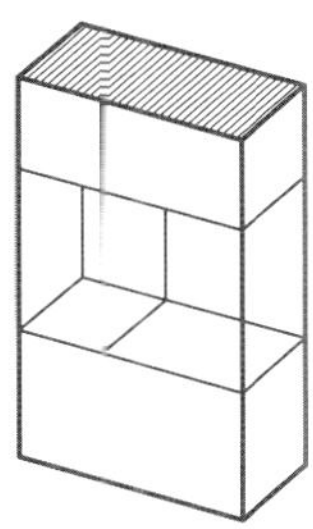

Display case unit

071 Domani

Coping with various lifestyles, the narrow space of the apartment is widened by turning two superimposed flats into a single duplex apartment. In particular, outside and inside spaces meet in an enlarged entrance with a doma (traditional entrance with dirt floor). There, visitors are greeted of and plants are watered and displayed.

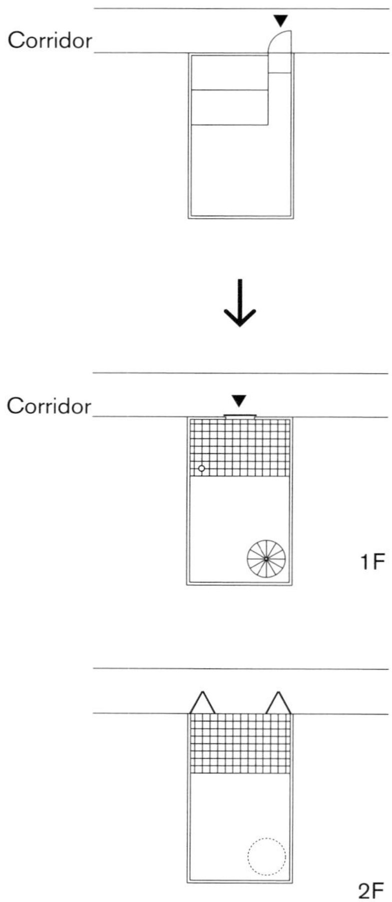

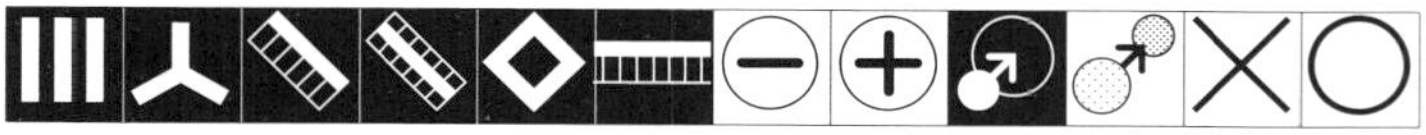

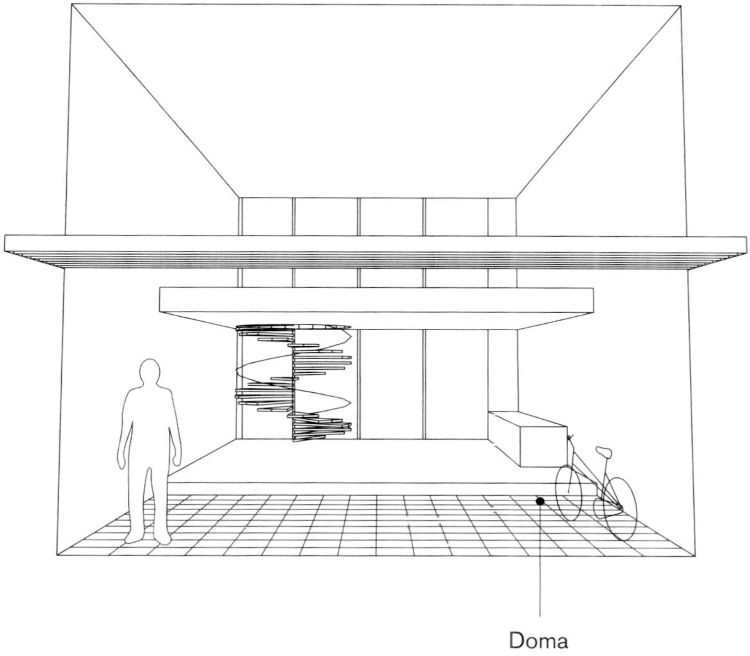
Doma

072
Foot On

Images of futons (traditional Japanese bed blankets) airing outside when the weather is nice, create a unique and peaceful atmosphere within the danchi. There are other times though when seeing them may be annoying for the neighboring environment. This system helps minimizing their visual impact by moving them to a horizontal position with a lever operated by foot. The angle of the apparatus can be adjusted according to the season in order to air the futon correctly.

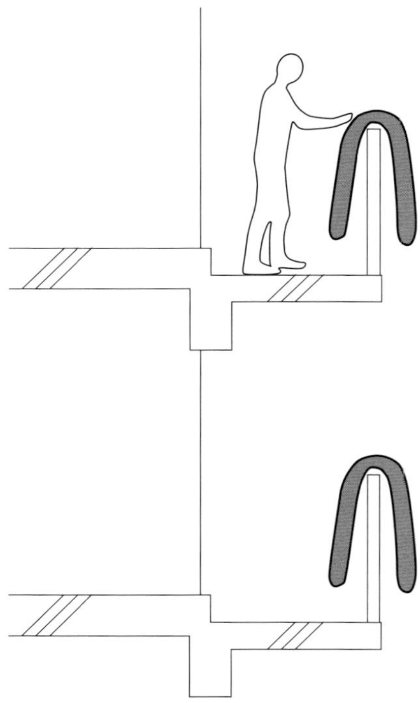

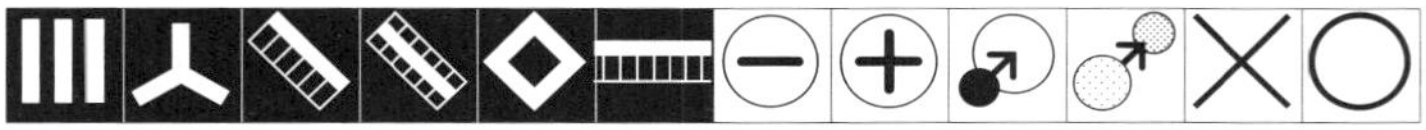

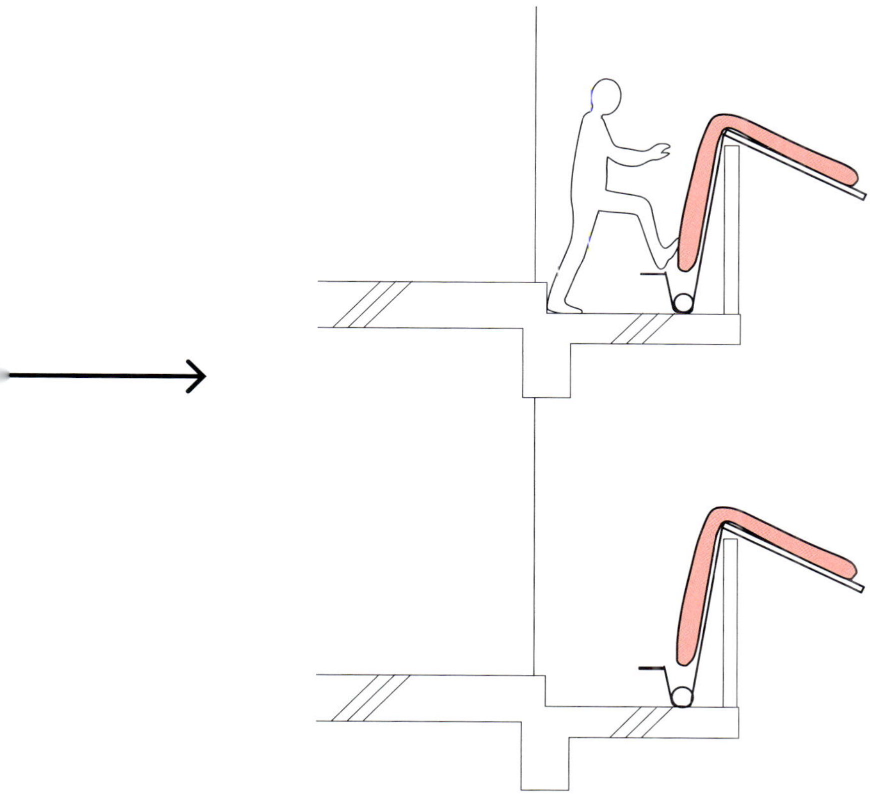

073
Foam Wall

This new system of partitioning is especially convenient when remodeling an apartment house. The panels, made of dense polyurethane foam, are easy to install for partitioning and storing as well. They are also easily cut, drilled, carved, and fixed against exterior walls providing good insulation material. In addition, they can be compressed prior packing and carrying.

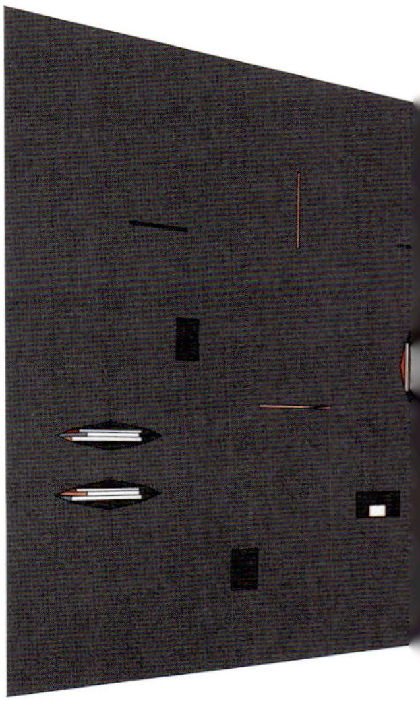

Product resembling a hard sponge

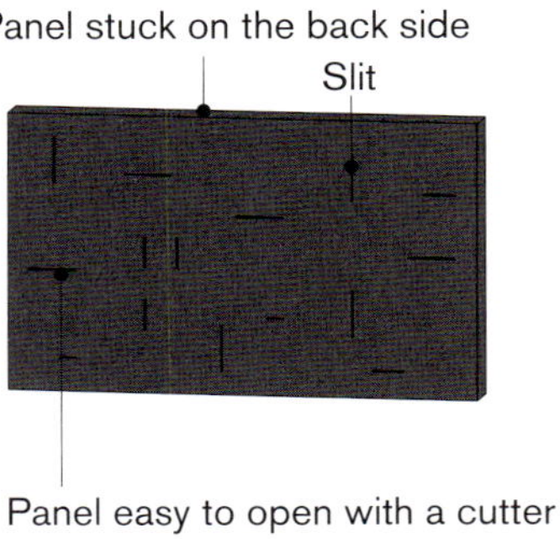

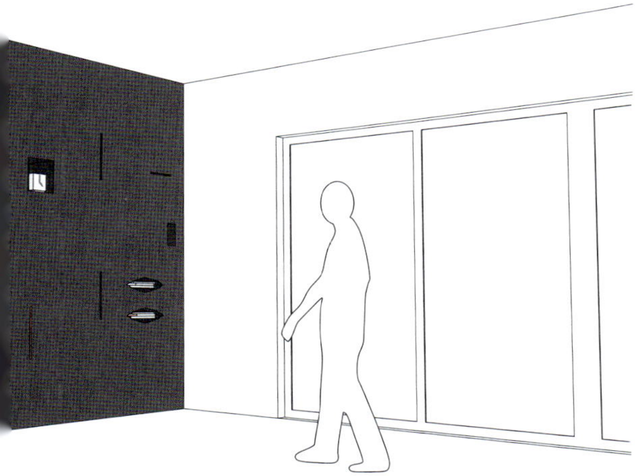

Various examples of use

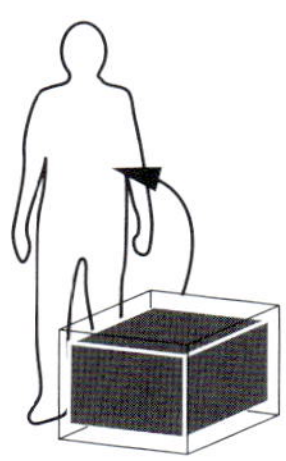

Compressed package
(swells naturally when opened)

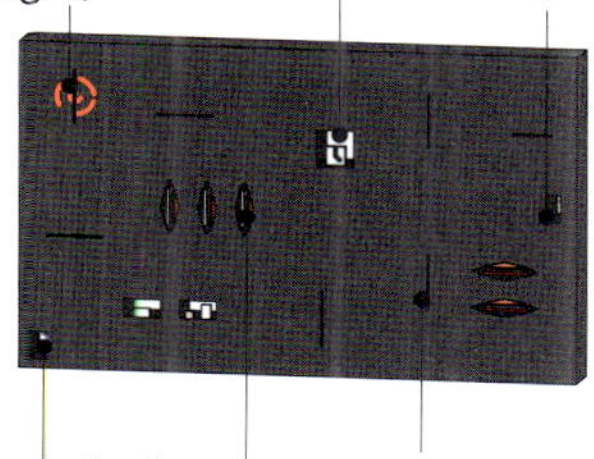

074 Fish Wall

A water tank used as an aquarium can also make a convenient partition for an apartment. Aquatic plants, goldfish, and tropical fish that inhabit the partition will bring a lively feeling to the stereotyped danchi apartments.

Partition made of water tanks

075
Peep Show

This system tries to take advantage of the cheap steel doors in the dark entrance room of the danchi apartments. A mini-projector fixed on the ceiling of the entrance projects, images taken outside by a CCD camera onto the existing door, which is painted white. Eventually, the darkness of the room becomes a positive condition for the projection. A TV projector could also be used.

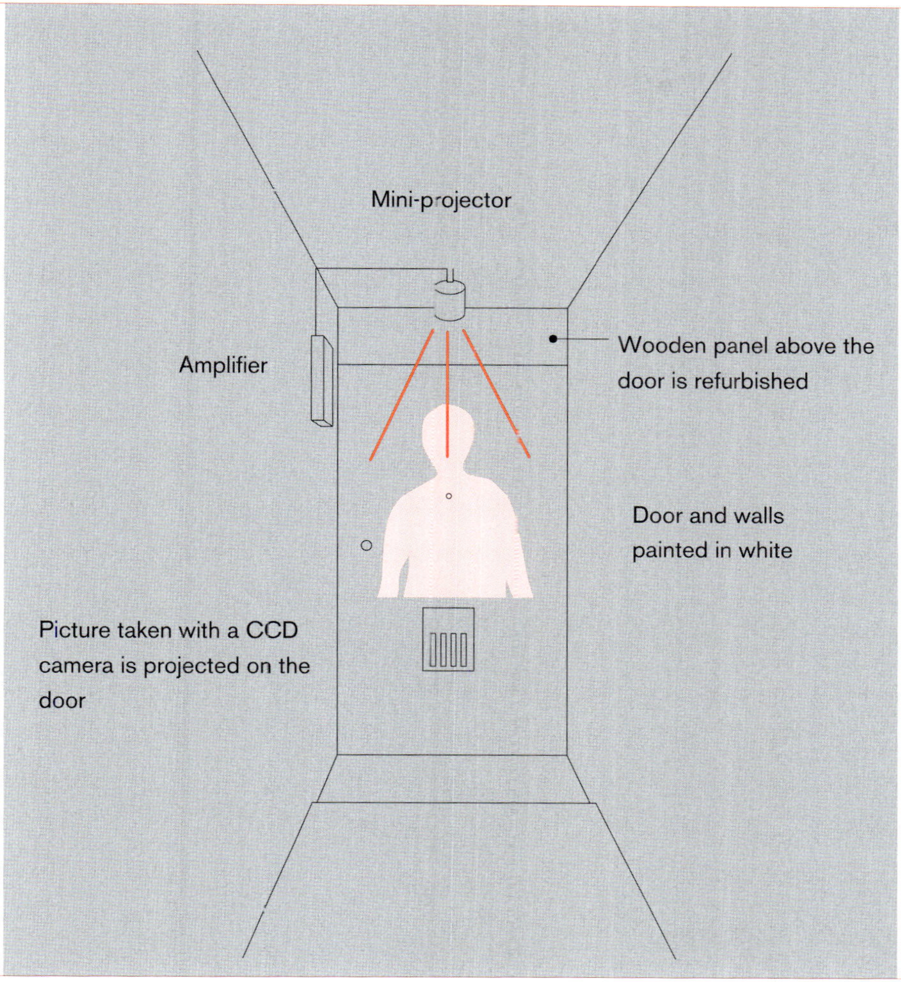
Mini-projector
Amplifier
Wooden panel above the door is refurbished
Door and walls painted in white
Picture taken with a CCD camera is projected on the door

076 Danchi Eye

Cameras are installed on the roof of the housing units of a high-rise danchi. From that viewpoint, they can film various scenes of the city. The data that are collected can be put together on the homepage www.danchi of the estate where other discussions about the revival plan and local information about the area are displayed. Information about the traffic situation of the metropolitan expressway, the weather, etc., can also be illustrated with the pictures taken by these observation cameras.

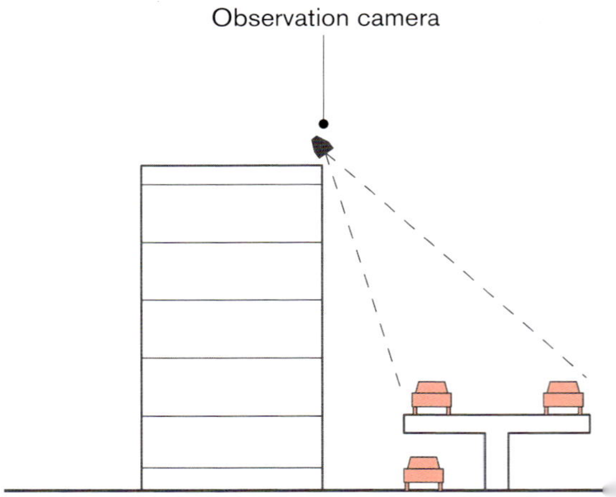

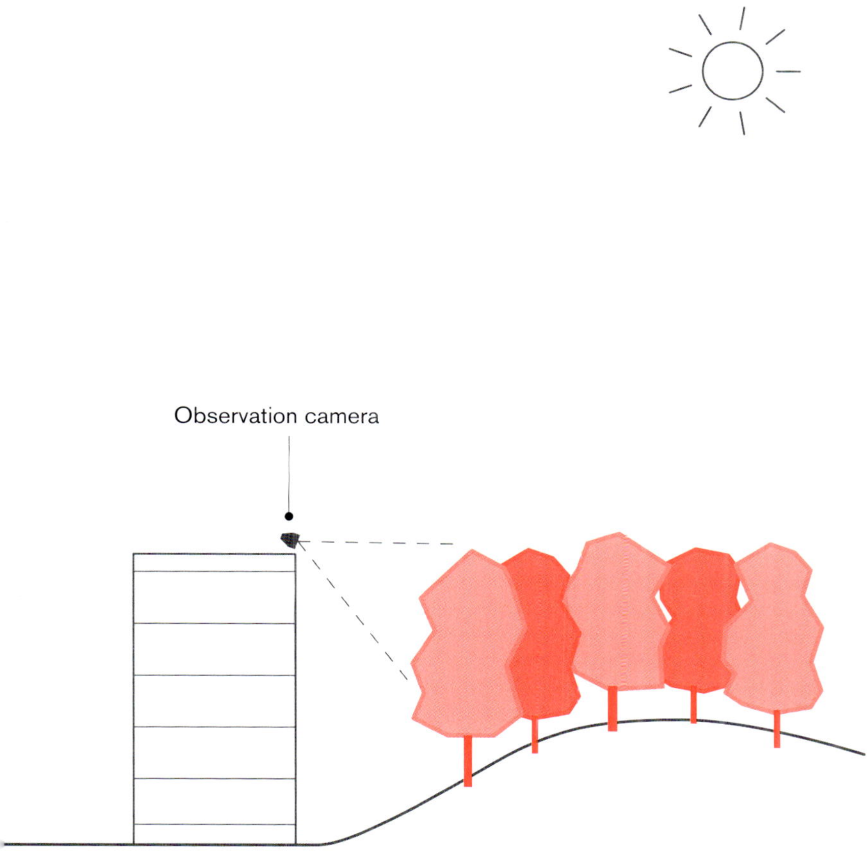
Observation camera

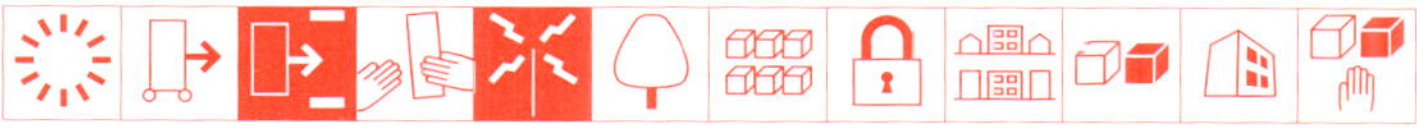

077 www.danchi

This website will help to establish and enrich the renovation catalogue made for saving the danchi. Images of various new estates gathered through the Internet may be included. Requests from the inhabitants of the many housing units are collected and entered into the data in order to quickly answer the demands. The site is also open to people other than the inhabitants of the danchi, though there are sections with more limited access. A chat corner with information reserved for the members of each particular estate has also been implemented.

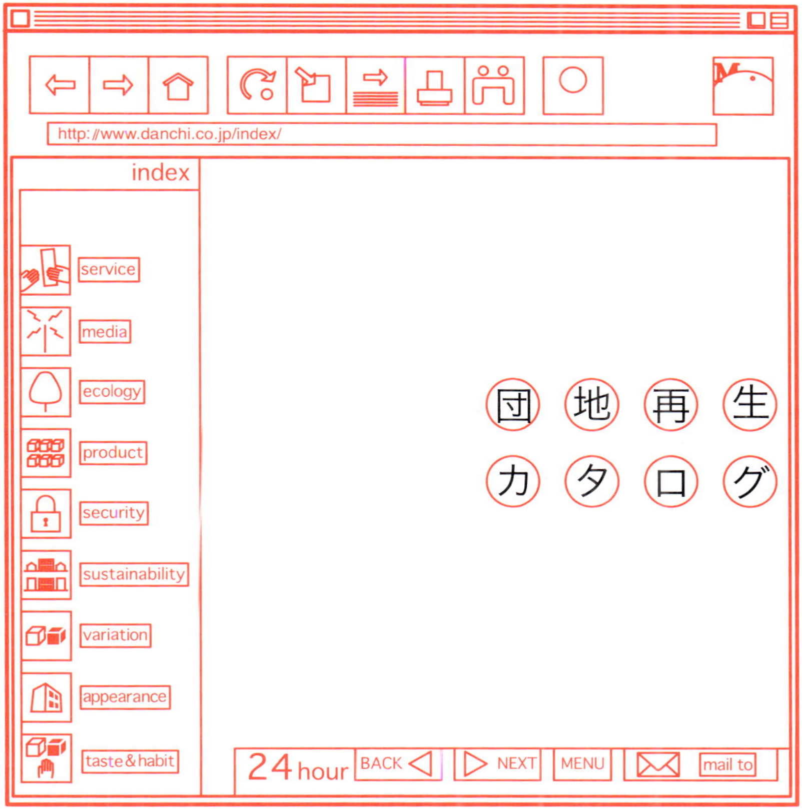
http://www.danchi.co.jp/index/
index
service
media
ecology
product
security
sustainability
variation
appearance
taste&habit
団 地 再 生
カ タ ロ グ
24 hour
BACK
NEXT
MENU
mail to

About MIKAN

Mikan is a Japanese-French architecture office based in Yokohama Japan. It was founded in 1995 by its present partners (Kiwako Kamo, Masashi Sogabe, Masayoshi Takeuchi, Manuel Tardits). Collaboraters: Kimihiko Tanaka, Hiroyuki Yoshioka

Mikan tries to go beyond disciplines. Its works range from large facilities in Japan and China, to schools, houses, and smaller-scale interior architecture and furniture. Mikan also participates in various exhibitions, workshops, artist-in-residence programs, and related installations.

Main works:
NHK broadcasting station in Nagano, Shibuya-Ax concert hall, Commercial facility Jian Wai Soho In Beijing, Toyota and France pavilions for the universal exhibition in Aichi 2005, shop for me Issey Miyake, renovation of the residence of the French embassy in Tokyo, pavilion for 150th anniversary of the foundation of Yokohama, Primary school in Ina, College in Akanedai.

Publications:
Mikan or its team of architects have published numerous books and articles.
Danchi Saisei Keikaku, Mikan Gumi no Renovation Catalogue, Inax Shuppan, 2001
(Original version in Japanese of the present book)
Architect's Works File Mikan , xknowledge, 2002
Ie no kioku (Memory of the House), Index Communications, 2003 (Japanese)
Post-office, Toto shuppan, 2006 (Japanese)
Architect's Works File Mikan2 , xknowledge, 2007
Tôkyô Fictions, Le Gac Press, 2011 (French, English), Kajima Shuppan (Japanese)

Acknowledgements:
The present book was made possible with a grant from the Japan Foundation. We are also extremely grateful to Philipp Sperrle from Jovis Publishers for his renewed confidence and trust beyond the deep and charming barrier of Japanese characters.

About MIKAN

The series a:p architektur:positionen is edited by
Christiane Fath and Jochen Visscher

The publication of this book was kindly supported by
The Japan Foundation

JAPANFOUNDATION

Based on the book Danchi Saisei Keikaku, Mikan Gumi no Renovation Catalogue first published in 2001 by Inax Shuppan, Tokyo.

Translation and introduction: Manuel Tardits, Yokohama
Design concept of the series a:p: Unverzagt Visuelle Kommunikation, Leipzig
Design and setting: Mikan
Printing and binding: fgb freiburger graphische betriebe

Bibliographic information published by the Deutsche Nationalbibliothek
The Deutsche Nationalbibliothek lists this publication in the Deutsche Nationalbibliografie; detailed bibliographic data are available on the Internet at http://dnb.d-nb.de

jovis Verlag GmbH
Kurfürstenstraße 15/16
10785 Berlin

www.jovis.de

ISBN 978-3-86859-085-2